Wood and Canvas Kayak Building

WOOD AND CANVAS
KAYAK BUILDING

George Putz

INTERNATIONAL MARINE

CAMDEN, MAINE

International Marine/
Ragged Mountain Press
A Division of The **McGraw·Hill** Companies

10   9   8   7

Library of Congress Cataloging-in-Publication Data

Putz, George.
   Wood & canvas kayak building / George Putz.
      p.   cm.
   Includes bibliographical references and index.
   ISBN 0-07-155939-6 (formally 0-87742-258-3)
      1. Kayaks—Design and construction. 2. Boatbuilding. I. Title.
   II. Title: Wood and canvas kayak building.
   VM353.P88 1990   90-4799
                                                                        CIP

Questions regarding the content of this book should be addressed to:

International Marine
P.O. Box 220
Camden, ME 04843

Questions regarding the ordering of this book should be addressed to:

The McGraw-Hill Companies
Customer Service Department
P.O. Box 547
Blacklick, OH 43004
Retail customers: 1-800-262-4729
Bookstores: 1-800-722-4726

Dedication

This book is dedicated to three people:

To James Putz, my brother, President of the San Francisco Bay Rowing Association, who not only believes but demonstrates that a good knife and a so-so screwdriver are tools enough for any job, including this one.

To Richard Williams (Edgar, Gweeka), fisherman and craftsman of Vinalhaven, Maine, who joined me building a few of these kayaks, and often came round the East Side in one to work on one.

To Victoria Louraina Dyer, my wife, town manager of Boothbay, Maine, whose future includes paddling kayaks in exotic places, beginning with this one.

Acknowledgments

All boatbuilders are very grateful for their customers; double gratitude here to Rick Stafford, friend, artist, photographer to the Fogg Museum at Harvard, sometime skipper of a 21-footer, and cover photographer for this book.

Sincere thanks also go to Gordon Lutz, friend, Director of Words and Pictures, inc., who in addition to always wanting one of these boats for himself and family, was able to find *his* photographs of curraghs.

Amazements go to Jon Eaton, Publisher at International Marine Publishing Company, who said to himself, "I've got this Great Idea; I'll let Putz write an Obscure Book about an Antiquated Boat built of Organic Materials!" To editor Heidi Brugger, of I.M.P., who made it all painless, thank you so very much.

Contents

Introduction

A FEW WORDS OF A KIND ABOUT SKIN BOATS

Skin-covered boats bring us close to the bone. You could say that *we* are skin boats of a sort, with our spine working as a flexible keel and, depending on habits of eating and exercise, more or less a full cargo. In fact, actual bones, usually from small whales, have been used for the ribs in the kayaks and umiaks of the Eskimos and Aleuts of the circumarctic, and quite probably in the coracles and curraghs of Ancient Europe, Great Britain, and Ireland. These are the craft most of us associate with skin-covered boats, but there are other types in use worldwide.

In this book I describe how to build and use a skin-covered kayak. The design of the kayak is one traditionally used by the Eskimos of southwestern Greenland. The designed lines of this boat were taken off an actual craft by the late Howard I. Chapelle, Curator of Transportation at Smithsonian Institution, and later rendered for occidental construction techniques by Norman L. Skene in the early 1920s. Skene, who was a well-known naval architect of the period, was an admirer of native craft, and his original article on this kayak, which appeared in the June, 1923 issue of *The Rudder,* made this boat very popular among home craftsmen and summer resort rusticators. (This article is reprinted in its entirety in Appendix A.)

His secret was simple: to propose using dimension-sawn wood instead of the native-carved driftwood and bone, and canvas covering instead of the traditional animal skins. The construction methods described here differ in three ways from those prescribed by Skene. They are more detailed, especially with regard to shop techniques and

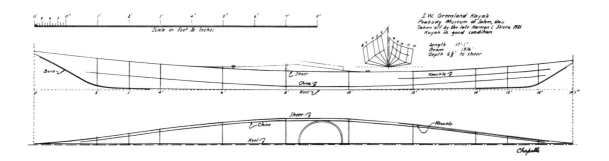

Figure 1-1. Skene's lines plans of the original native craft, as they appear in Adney and Chappelle's *Skin Boats and Bark Canoes of North America* and on which the boats in this book are based. REPRINTED BY PERMISSION OF THE SMITHSONIAN INSTITUTION.

options; they take advantage of modern adhesives, epoxies, and so reduce the number of screw fastenings required; and they include information that permits this same design to be made larger or smaller than the original 17-footer, at the wishes of the builder, through the use of a pocket calculator.

The two kayaks shown under construction in the photographs and drawings in this book are taken from the same set of lines and offsets (see Chapter 3). The forms for the larger boat, however, were increased in all dimensions 18 percent, as if for a 21-footer, but spaced a bit closer together to create a relatively shorter boat (18 ½ feet) suitable for rowing as well as paddling. The 17-foot version is exactly as prescribed by Skene. The 18 ½-foot version is included to show how the original may be altered to suit personal needs and tastes.

Kayaks are splendid boats. Light, fast, easy to build, inexpensive, transportable, and good-looking, these craft have a history going back at least 2,000 years. They are much more capable than presumed common sense or ordinary nautical prejudice might lead you to expect. Not only have the natives of the Arctic used them in open-ocean fishing and hunting of large sea mammals for millennia, but thousands of Americans have come to make ocean kayaking one of the fastest growing outdoor sports in recent times. Though the construction techniques described here create a boat that is lighter and not so powerful as that used by Arctic natives, nor as durable and strong as the fiberglass craft generally used by whitewater and ocean-kayaking sportsmen, wood frame and canvas kayaks are utterly serviceable and, on open water, capable of withstanding all of the ordinary demands of kayak utility and sport alike. The important difference here is one of aesthetics, the use of natural materials in a beautiful, traditional craft designed for open water.

If your purpose is to possess and use a kayak for white water, so-called slalom work on rivers, this is not your boat! Even the fiberglass or carbon-fiber/Kevlar optional construction methods suggested later on in the book do not make this type of kayak suitable for fast river use; the inevitable bumps and scrapes that attend running rapids destroy canvas-covered surfaces. In any case the sharp angular shape of these boats at the keel and chine makes them "track"—i.e., go in a straight line—much too well to allow the maneuverability that river-running demands. These are open-water boats that prefer lakes and the sea.

I should mention here, by the way, that the word *kayak* is spelled several ways in English-language nautical literature, but that we will stick with this one. In British English most of the books and articles written about "canoeing" are in fact about kayaking, for the word *canoe* originally entered the English language via Spanish, from the ship logs of Columbus, who got it from Caribbean Indians, meaning "boat." What Americans call a canoe, the English call a Canadian canoe, with emphasis on the "Canadian." In this book I follow American practice, reserving *canoe* to designate a full-bodied, double-ended, deckless boat, and *kayak* to refer to relatively longer and lower decked, double-ended boats. I have to indulge this little discussion about terminology only because some of the best kayaking literature in print comes from England, and they call these boats canoes!

Skin-covered boats, including kayaks, developed in places where there was not adequate timber available to allow fabrication of boats completely of wood, nor the metal or metallurgy required to properly fasten nautical craft that was completely of wood timber construction. The kayaks of the circumarctic reflect such conditions. In winter all is snow and ice. In summer there are thousands of square miles of open, treeless tundra, ice-scrubbed rocky shores, and the open sea. In this desolate environment the only wood available is that carried down the great rivers of the North from the far interior by violent spring floods,

Figure 1-2. Part of a fleet of seven curraghs making off to Inishmore in the Arran Islands to meet the ferry boat and take off passengers and cargoes. The island has no wharves for large ships so all transport is by skin-covered (canvas) boat, as it has been for 2,000 years. © GORDON LUTZ

which disgorge the driftwood into the sea, which in turn churns and washes it before, finally, depositing it on the lonely beaches where it is gathered by the natives for all of their wood needs. Metal was not entirely unavailable before contact with white Europeans—there were natural surface copper deposits here and there—but it was very rare and much too precious to use in boats. Instead, leather thongs of seal, walrus, and caribou hide were used to bind boat frames together.

With these fundamental simple materials the Eskimo and Aleut built, and some continue to build (even if for museum curators), strong, seaworthy kayaks that are light—can be carried or sledded by one person—and capable of long sea passages in waters notorious for fickle weather and dangerous marine conditions. Indeed, there is a recorded case of a Greenland native who, working offshore for halibut, was caught in a gale and weeks later cast ashore on the Scottish Hebrides, alive. Light, strong, and capable: These characteristics make them fine craft for the Eskimo and for the contemporary craftsperson who wants the same features in a personal boat, self-built on a small budget.

In a sense, a prospective boatbuilder with limited funds is in the same predicament as the Arctic native. Long lengths of clear, boat-grade lumber are difficult to find and expensive when available. Similarly, fastenings—the screws, boatnails, or rivets in larger sizes used to fasten wooden boats—have become prohibitively expensive. And, when you have completed a wooden boat, even a small one, you typically have a boat that is too heavy for one person to pick up, that is difficult to move, and that ordinarily requires docks, moorings, and trailers for its berthing and transport—all added and continuing expenses. Furthermore, a heavier boat is a slower boat and, when undecked and in small size, a much less seaworthy boat, for heavy boats must plow through the water rather than glide over it. A kayak, by contrast, rides like a duck over the waves, not through them, as do most rowboats. Finally, a kayak sits low in the water and presents less surface to the wind, allowing much more control of the boat in windy conditions, a feature appreciated by anyone who has been caught out while rowing in a breeze. This is not to criticize rowboats too much. Along with canoeing and kayaking, rowing is a wonderful activity and its good boats things of beauty.

There is, of course, a philosophy and point of view here. People who choose to build their own boat of natural materials do not do so because it is necessarily practical. The same energy and time spent building a boat could be spent earning the money to go out and purchase a boat that is made of more durable materials and is ready to

Figure 1-3. These lads row along and so show us some curragh construction details. Ribs and stringers make up the framework, over which canvas is laid, the weave being "filled" or "killed" and sealed with ordinary tar. © GORDON LUTZ

use immediately, perhaps with some cash to spare. To build one's own craft is to trade a certain kind of practicality for personal satisfaction. And to build with natural materials is also in a way to make a statement about yourself and how you want to relate to the world—to be thought of as part of the world, rather than an imposition on it. Boats made of natural materials have a way of mellowing and becoming more beautiful with time and care. What the boating industry touts to be the disadvantages of natural materials are, from my point of view, advantages. True, they require maintenance, but in the discipline of maintenance they generate a personal relationship. Under abuse they can break; with neglect they decay, but they also engender care. The occasional repair deepens one's understanding of the being of the boat. A boat that you build yourself of wood and canvas becomes part of you. That it shares our human weakness, mortality, is a good thing, not a bad one.

Anyway, the notion that modern boat construction materials are immortal is baldly stupid. Everything breaks and is eventually thrown away—and even morons these days come to understand that there is no "away." Broken fiberglass never rots, but it does oxidize under sunlight; the tiny pieces that flake off become smaller and smaller until, as they approach the molecular level, they are ingested along with oceanic nutrients by the phyto- and zooplankton that constitute the bottom of the oceanic food chain. Scientists cannot yet predict what the consequences of this ingested material will be. Plastics and resins are appearing in an ever-increasing number of plankton samples. When the career of a wood and canvas kayak ends, it becomes plain, good soil or marine nutrients again.

As attitudes bring people to a project like this one, attitudes have a direct bearing on the outcome. Kayaks do not as a rule last very long. Ten years is a reasonable lifespan. I know of a couple of craft that are forty or fifty years old, but these are framed in yellow pine, well oiled, and so have survived several recanvasings through eras when canvas duck was readily available. More care and foresight during the building process will yield a longer-lived boat, but the primary advantage of this project is that, for a relatively modest investment, an unskilled woodworker may acquire a pleasurable boat quite rapidly. Chapter 8 on maintenance, repair, and diseases of canvas-covered boats will aid toward a practical longevity.

The editors and I have strived to make the discussion and instructions for building this kayak as clear and complete as possible. But, some readers may get the kayak bug and want to know more, especially with regard to how native peoples of the North built and used their kayaks. Homework for these readers should include the wonderful work of David Zimmerly, Ethnographer at the Museum of Civilization, in Ottawa, Canada. He has devoted his career to documenting the basic types of native kayaks of the circumarctic, not merely describing them, but living with the last of the old native builders and recording the entire construction process from the collection of materials to launching and use. He has also redesigned native craft for contemporary shop practice, similar to the techniques described here. His publications are described in Chapter 9.

Space, Tools, and Materials

2

THE SHOP

Workshops, working spaces, are very special places. The designation might also include studios, kitchens, studies, offices, and libraries, but here we must refer to a place specifically designated for woodworking, the use of woodworking shop tools, and all the noise and messes to which this nomenclature applies. Since a workshop is a place where new things are brought into being, where the world is both materially and spiritually increased, the workshop should be considered a sanctuary.

This kayak building project presupposes that you have a basic kit of hand and power-hand tools, and an appropriate space in which to set up the boat, handle and manipulate materials during inclement weather, and be reasonably assured that you can put something down and find it still there when next you reach for it. Obviously, a boatbuilding shop or shed is best. A home woodworking shop is very good. A garage, mess area, or studio is adequate. In many parts of the country, and during some seasons, you can set up outdoors, covering the work with a sheet of plastic or tarpaulin at night, during work hiatuses, rainstorms, and fog.

Some how-to articles and books of times past claimed that any old place is satisfactory, and a bottom bureau drawer of inexpensive, probably bubble-packed tools is adequate for work such as this. They would show people extracting their boats out of third-floor kitchen windows to prove it. In the face of this depraved suggestion, the illustrative art for such published advice inevitably showed the writer's

shop to be fully equipped, beautifully lighted, neat as a pin, and secured like a bank! The shop in which I built the kayaks used to illustrate this book is an old wagon shed attached as an ell to an 80-year-old farmhouse on the coast of Maine. Finished in yellow pine matchboard, the place was very dark. On the ceiling of this cave I mounted four three-bulb 40-inch fluorescent light fixtures with lenses that I bought from a commercial wrecker who at the time was tearing down an old warehouse. This workshop is the average sort for my area, which has an especially dense population of jacks-of-all-trades: inshore small-boat fishermen who are accustomed to doing their own work, woodworking and boatbuilding included.

The *sanctuary* aspect of your working space must be emphasized. If it is not an official workshop, and woodworking only an occasional or even first-time activity, then you must be able to secure your work area with a lock. Otherwise, the casual tool-borrowing habits of friends and the ordinary presumptive behavior of family will haunt the project. Absolutely insist on the inviolacy of your workshop and everything in it! They may not respect you in the morning, but your

Figures 2-1 and 2-2.
Views from the front
and back of the shop—
otherwise known as the
cave. The powered surface
planer is necessary in my
area since commercial
custom wood suppliers do
not constitute a local
infestation. The large
band saw is not used in
this project, so you can
relax.

work surface and tools will remain available on an as-needed basis.

Your working space required to build the 17-foot kayak should be no less than 21 feet long by 6 feet wide. If your workbench is to be placed alongside the setup of the boat, then the space must be wider. The point is to be easily able to walk completely around the setup and to stoop and crouch along its entire length without snagging, bumping, or fouling body, feet, head, equipment, or electrical cords.

Create the very best lighting you can. Well-lighted work goes better, faster, and is much less tiring. To good ceiling-mounted light fixtures add at least one movable, housed mechanic's light on a long cord for intense illumination of detailed work. Readers who live in rural areas and northern climate will want a reliable heat source during winter, though a "room-temperature" space is often too warm for much of the woodworking, which requires lots of effort in the arms and upper body. I like a shop in the mid-50s, Fahrenheit. This kayak requires a lot of walking back and forth between the workbench and setup, so a wood floor and high-quality shoes with good arch support are an advantage.

TOOLS

The following discussion details the kit of basic tools generally required for the project, but these ought to be supplemented with a few additional tools that sometimes will make the difference between a pleasure and a chore. As in the rest of life, more is usually better, but adequate is enough. You can beg, borrow, or rent the conveniences if purchase is out of the question. Meanwhile, here are the basics:

Your Work Surfaces

You need a bench on which to work, not necessarily a workbench *per se*. The classic woodworker's bench with all its fancy vises and accoutrements has very little utility in constructing these boats. All of the primary wooden members are either long thin strips, unmanageable on a regular bench, or small, oddly shaped pieces that do not require a large bench. A small, stoutly constructed table or wall-mounted bench, two feet by three feet in dimension or larger, is adequate.

The bench should be mounted with a vise. The usual flush front- or side-mounted woodworker's vises are the least desirable for our use. A top-mounted, revolving metalworking or engineer's vise is better, especially if the jaws are tapped for screws or bolts by which you can attach your own shaped-up wooden jaws (preferably of hardwood). As you will see in some of the illustrations (Figure 4–5a, for example), I often use the splendid General Tool Company's swivel vise, which not only swivels as a unit but has swivel jaws as well, allowing the vise to accept oddly shaped pieces. It is the ideal vise for this, though its price has become prohibitive in recent years. But do not become discouraged because you don't have a Big Deal vise. Any regular top-mounted bench vise will do just fine.

You will want a pair of stout sawhorses, a broom, and at least two stools, one of which is height-adjustable. Experienced woodworkers and carpenters know the value of sound sawhorses. Avoid the temptation to use the sheetmetal brackets made for 2 × 4s ordinarily offered at the hardware store. Even if you could find real 2 × 4s today, which you cannot do, they make inferior wobbly things, useful in house carpentry only. Sawhorses will be used early in the project for laying out and sawing the forms and again in the second half of the construction when they support the kayak frame after it has come off the forms. Inexperienced woodworkers should take special pains to build their own sawhorses. The effort will provide experience and a sense of confidence with the tools.

Have a good broom on hand and use it often. Without regular

sweeping your work space soon becomes an environment where tools and fastenings disappear, and the quality of your workmanship becomes shoddy. There is a rule of thumb that states: The smaller the pieces of wood you use in construction (of anything), the larger the scrap, sawdust, and chip pile you create. Kayak construction is a good demonstration of this principle, especially if you get out—i.e., saw— your own wood stock to the sizes called for in this book. Kayak builders who live in rural and suburban localities should know that plants such as roses and strawberries respond well to woodchip mulches.

A couple of seating stools are very useful. Much of the fitting, drilling, and fastening on these craft is done in a half-standing or stooping position, hard on the back while bending over and bad knews for the knees when kneeling. A short-legged stool (preferably a three-legged one) is a real back-saver. It serves both as a sitting place for mid-height work and as a local bench on which to keep fastenings, drill, drivers, glue, and so on close at hand. If possible, you should also have one or more adjustable stools in the shop space. Much of boatbuilding is composed of looking and head-scratching; even full-time pro-fessional boatbuilders will tell you this. A short stool will allow you to relax a bit yet keep you local to the work, up and ready to carry on in ways that a chair over in the corner does not. Also, friends and the idle curious will stop by to watch, kibitz, and chat while you work. It is best to have these lookers-on seated in a prescribed place, rather than to allow them to wander about getting underfoot and picking up critical tools and materials. As a general rule, remember that while you are doing something in your shop, those looking on are not doing anything. Since we remain a nation with Puritan roots, those who are not doing anything feel jealousy and envy toward those who are working. Unconsciously, inadvertently, they will detract from your work. Be friendly and improve their lives by keeping them in their place, out of the way, on a stool. So much for shop space equipment.

More Tools

Even a most abbreviated list of basic tools required for woodworking will seem unreasonably long to a prospective woodworker who has no tools. At today's prices, the basic kit of hand and powered hand tools will come approximately to twice the cost of the materials required to build this kayak. But, you have the satisfaction of knowing that it is a one-time investment. Good tools will last several lifetimes, most importantly yours. In fact, it will pay you to look up dealers in used tools in the telephone directory. Most metropolitan areas have at least one such dealer—and you should visit him before you purchase new tools from hardware or department stores or mail-order outlets. Very good tools are available in this country, but there was a slippage in domestic tool quality from the end of World War II until the early 1970s. Tool kits assembled before this time are still in use, so a visit to secondhand tool dealers is very worthwhile.

By good tools I mean tools that are made of good quality soft steel, have a burnished look, and take an edge quickly yet hold the edge for a relatively long time. Stainless steel, for example, is seldom appropriate. Good tools feel right. They have a balance and heft that is comfortable and somehow natural in the hand when you pick them up. Generally, good tools have an attractive finish. If the manufacturer or previous owner took observable and feelable care in the tool, then it is a sign that perhaps you should also.

The tools required for setting up, getting out the forms, establishing a centerline, and erecting and plumbing the forms are: a framesquare, a chalkline, a yardstick, and a small bubble level.

Since almost all of the hammering required in the building of this kayak is light, a smaller 9- to 11-ounce claw hammer is generally to be preferred over the standard 13-ounce size. Once you own one of the lighter ones, you will be surprised at how often you will pick it up in preference to the larger one for many odd jobs around the household. Also, a plastic or hard rubber/plastic-headed hammer of medium size will be useful. It is more gentle on wood surfaces than a steel-headed one, and again you will discover many domestic uses for the tool beyond this project. Except for a couple of procedures, the hammering called for in this book is limited to nudging, fitting, and aligning. A bigger hammer is not a better hammer.

You will need a bevel and a compass. An ordinary woodworker's bevel is not necessary; in fact it is a handicap in most boat work because it is excessively thick and does not give a good line against flat surfaces, and almost always requires two hands in the work. In boat work, one hand is often needed to hold a piece of wood on which you wish to strike the bevel line, and the appearance of a boatbuilder striking a bevel line with a pencil in his teeth is common around boatyards. A better tool is created if you simply true up a couple of pieces of thin hardwood laths and screw or bolt them together so that they will adjust with firm thumb pressure and then hold the angle. A compass is a compass, but the larger woodworker's variety, 10 or more inches long, is preferred, with a large, stout locking wingnut that loosens and tightens easily but reliably.

Screwdrivers are made in several classic patterns, and it is strictly a matter of personal preference which to choose, so long as the steel at the tip is of good quality. Avoid plastic handles. Unless you have tough working hands, mechanic's screwdrivers cause blisters in the occasional fastening marathons that this kayak presents. Since nearly all of the screws in the boat are of the same head size, and the cost of the relatively small screwdriver minor in the total project budget, it is a good idea to custom-grind the tip of your screwdriver so that it completely fills the screw slot. This will help prevent slippage out of the slot and reduce the attendant damage to wood and canvas in the vicinity of the screw. Incidentally, keep a piece of candle or paraffin wax on the bench or service stool. By scraping the screw threads once quickly through a piece of wax before driving, you will find the job of driving is made much easier, the onset of ratchet-wrist is delayed, and you get a better seal between the fastening and the wood. Some people have become dependent on power screwdrivers, or the Versamat attachment for electric drills, and I will agree that they are godsends for projects involving larger, tougher stock. But the wood in these boats is so small, light, and soft that the occasional slippage you always get with electric drivers could cause trouble, particularly after the canvas has been stretched over the frame. On this kayak, screwdriving by hand is best.

You need saws. In this project you may get by with ordinary crosscut, rip, and coping saws, but an improved combination includes a small backsaw (sometimes called a dovetailing saw), and a bow- or stretchersaw (available at quality woodworking tool outlets). Again, the wood pieces in the boat are relatively small, and many of the longer saw cuts called for are curved. So, the backsaw is more comfortable and practical than a standard crosscut saw for the many small, light cuts, and the bowsaw is able to track more reliably than a coping saw on the curved lines occasionally prescribed. An ordinary hand ripsaw comes into play only toward the end of the project, when you must get out your coamings. If you intend to do all of the construction exclusively with hand tools, you will have to rip out the stringers, an effort involving 180 feet of ripping! Your age, philosophy, and notions about heroism will participate in this decision. We don't presume to advise. . . . The hell we don't: Cut stringers on a standing power saw or have them commercially cut and planed to dimension. Only you and God will know. . . .

Other hand tools required are: Coarse and fine woodworker's rasps in good cutting condition, one side rounded, the other flat, and the whole tapered; a smoothing plane; a drawknife; a spokeshave; and a sharp knife. Of course, you will need sharpening stones, to grind and hone cutting edges, and a leather strop for finish sharpening. An old leather belt will do. From the very start you should have the best sharpening stones you can afford, in at least two grades of coarseness. Think of them as the most important tools in your shop. Before anything else, learn to make cutting edges sharp. The activity is a pleasurable one, never onerous. *Planecraft,* distributed in this country by Woodcraft Supply Company (see Chapter 9 for ordering information and price), is a book that will free you from the life of frustration and impotence led by those without the ability to "get the edge."

An interesting alternative to the drawknife is the so-called crooked knife, offered by the North West Company (see Appendix B for address and ordering information). For 350 years it was a primary trade good in the North American fur trade, and it has been a pivotal tool in many Indian crafts, most especially canoe building. These crooked knife blades used to come unhafted, but once you got a handle on them they were excellent for splitting, shaping, scraping, and numerous other tasks. (They now come with handle.) In times past, a crooked knife was, in one blade, the Swiss Army Knife of half a continent!

You cannot have too many clamps in medium and small sizes. C-clamps are the usual requirement, but so-called guitar clamps, which are soft-jawed and cam-acting, are very effective on projects using small pieces of wood. For safety's sake, goggles, face mask, and ear protectors are indicated for some operations, especially if you are going to use standing power tools. *When using power tools always wear safety equipment!*

This hand-tool part of the kit is rounded out with a regular bench square, a two-foot folding ruler, and a pencil and an ear onto which to place it. Hint: Always remember to remove the pencil from your ear at workday's end. Otherwise, it is doomed to extinction in the special hell reserved for all pencils brought into the house. Save a pencil. Put it in plain sight on the workbench. Then, lock up the shop.

The issue of what power tools are needed is more ambiguous for the simple reason that none is absolutely required. But, several are very handy to have—lost chuck keys, frayed cords, burnt brushes, armatures, and coils, exhausted storage batteries notwithstanding. To wit:

For cutting out the forms, and ripping out the keelson, keel, stringers, and bilge and gunwale strips, a power circular saw is a blessing. (These parts of the boat will be described and illustrated in the next chapter.) For drilling and countersinking, a quarter-inch or three-eighths-inch power drill is a constant companion. Good cordless models are recommended. For getting out the curved cuts on the stems and floor timbers, a power bayonet saw is a time-saver, and, when it comes time to build the paddles (or oars), a power hand plane and both reciprocal and beltsanders are wonderful.

But, here we are with a list of six powered hand tools and I haven't even mentioned the genuine utility of a small or medium-sized table saw, a small band saw, and stationary jointer and sander! Yes, friends, for only $2,000 in tools, you can build a cheap boat! You may borrow tools, but that ends in lost friendships. Or, you may rent a kit of powered hand tools by the week. All metropolitan areas have industrial rental agencies, and their rates are good. Most rental outfits offer a rent/lease/purchase arrangement, so if you become emotionally attached to a particular tool your rental money may be applied toward its purchase at a wholesale or "secondhand" price. Rental is definitely worth checking out. Otherwise, a power drill is the only electrical tool especially recommended. Certainly, a boat made entirely by handwork, without power tools, would be an object of personal pride, *par excellence!* Buy a drill!

MATERIALS

The framework of this kayak is composed entirely of wood, fastened with glue and screws. You may, if you wish, eliminate the glue. However, modern adhesives are so good that their lasting security is undeniable, and the doubling of the screw-fastening called for when glue is dispensed with increases the expense and difficulty of the craft, and probably compromises its safety. Use the glue!

Some wood philosophy: Most any construction-grade wood may be used in the construction of this kayak, but consider the following thoughts.

Most treatises, books, and articles about boatbuilding are too precious and patronizing for our purposes here. They emphasize the tremendous strain that the sea places on boats. They harp on getting long, clear pieces of expensive wood species and grades, that bend easily, can be glued and fastened effectively, resist rot, do not corrode fastenings, and are beautiful. It is the magic world of clear white pasture oak, old-growth pine, deep-swamp Eastern white cedar, longleaf pine and proprietary cypress, exotic mahoganies, butternut, Sitka spruce, Port Orford cedar, and other species whose aristocratic bloodlines endanger integrity in woodshops from St. Johns to Hobart.

Well, our kayak looks like a boat, acts like a boat, and is a boat, but building it is not boatbuilding in the usual sense. The structure of these boats is more like bridge- or trestlework than like ordinary boat construction. Furthermore, these craft are not (or, rather, should not be) left in the water. Their natural disposition is to be stored indoors, used for short periods, and then dried out and stored again.

So, pine, spruce, or cedar of local variety is just fine for the entire construction. The very lightest, strongest-by-weight, and fanciest construction would be entirely of airplane-grade spruce, using the best epoxy glue available and double-screwing all joints. I don't, nor do I recommend this. I choose wood that is acceptable and available, and after that in accordance with what sort of person orders the boat and where and how the craft is to be used. My efforts range from a very light 17-footer in cedar with knots left in unscarfed and unbutted, to a 21-foot monster, all of quarter-sawn oak butted, reinforced, and overspecified everywhere. Inshore recreational paddler, and intrepid offshore nature photographer were alike well served without recourse to boatbuilding religion.

If you live near a good lumberyard or sawmill where you can actually find a sympathetic and accommodating ear, I strongly recommend getting full-length strips of clear cedar, pine, or spruce, plus two planks of the same wood out of which to cut your floor timbers, deck beams, stems, knees, and carlins. Generally, softwoods are lighter than hardwoods, and softwoods also usually bend and twist more easily than do hardwoods. Exceptions are longleaf yellow pine, which should be considered a hardwood, and white ash, which is hardy and behaves in the shop like a softwood in the way it bends and twists easily, especially if green or wet. If you cannot get clear strips, get unclear ones in extra length so that you can cut out the weak places and scarf. If full lengths are impossible or too expensive for your taste, get strips that are longer than half-length and scarf all of them. Indeed, if it comes down to it, you can take an ax, wedges, gluts, and a sledgehammer and split out everything you need from cordwood— don't laugh! Except that I used a large band saw (and a chainsaw in earlier times), all my coamings and several stems have come from firewood piles! How else these days is one to get maple, ash, oak, cherry, hickory, locust, and hornbeam nearly for free?

The closer that you can get your delivered wood to finished required dimension, the more you save in time, effort, wear and tear on tools, and patience. If you can turn around and pick up a piece of wood you need—except for final shaping—you can complete one of these boats in a week of working days. If you have to saw out and finish all your own stock to dimension, it will be more nearly a month. It's the old time-versus-money equation.

Several kinds of wood were used to construct the particular boats photographed in this book. The various parts of the kayak are described and illustrated in the next chapter, but for the purposes of considering the wood stock I used; the boats have quarter-sawn ash keelsons and keels (the strips on the center-bottom, inside and outside the canvas skin). The stringers, chines, and gunwales are of Eastern white cedar, reinforced at knots and weak places with glued butt blocks. The floor timbers and deck beams are of the same cedar, as are the deck stringers and carlins. The stem knees, both forward and aft, are of red oak that I cut out of an old bureau drawer I found on the dump—probably a hundred years old, and so very well seasoned. The coamings are a colorful combination maple, ash, apple, and walnut, all from the dump and woodpile scroungings. The rails were ripped from a mahogany plank I purchased at a boatyard. As you might guess, there is a certain challenge to, and fun in, studying and scrounging wood. The price of not rising to the challenge is of course a higher price.

The Parts of a Kayak / Getting Out the Form

3

Many people make a hobby of studying and collecting boat plans. Of the 150 or so periodicals devoted to recreational boating and yachting published in the English-speaking world, few omit a plans section for their readers to study and enjoy. It tends to be a lifetime interest, and no wonder, for boats have an infinite variety of forms and subtlety. The initiated may want simply to scan the next several paragraphs, but those new to the terminology of boat construction and design will have a much easier time appreciating the whys and wherefores of the construction procedures that are described later if they carefully read this summary of the basics.

BOAT PARTS

Boats have fronts, backs, tops, bottoms, and sides. Only the bottom and sides are called by those names, and even they are divided into different areas with specialized names. Fronts are *bows,* and backs are *sterns.* In the case of light, double-ended craft such as our kayaks, bow and stern are referred to collectively as *stems,* a term that in conventional boatbuilding usually refers to the timbers that underlie only the bow. The top of the boat is the *deck.* Obviously, boats must go through the water, and the less a boat disturbs the water as it moves through it, the more efficiently the boat performs. Bottoms have several different parts that affect the water and the boat in different ways. The area of the boat that parts the water at the bow is the *cutwater* or *entrance.* The widest part of the boat is the *beam,* and the area between the entrance and the beam is the *forebody.* The area of the bottom from the beam to where the boat leaves the water at the stern is the *run*. There is a curve or angle where the boat emerges from the water at the sides; this is the *bilge*. In the case of hard-angled craft such as our kayak, it is more often called the *chine*. The *draft* is the depth at which a boat sits in the water, and the angle between the bottom-most part of the boat, called the *keel*, and the chines is called the *deadrise*. Finally, the bottom terminology is rounded out with the amount a keel bends upward toward the ends from the beam (or *amidships*), and this is the *rocker*. These parts are indicated in Figure 3–1.

Before naming the rest of the boat, we should consider some of the affects that bottom proportions have on performance. The weight of a boat is the *displacement,* so called because water is pushed aside or displaced when the boat floats. The more water displaced, the more energy required to move the boat through the water at a given speed. Keep in mind, too, that the passenger (s) and cargo aboard a boat when underway are part and parcel of the effective displacement of the boat.

As a boat moves, a *bow wave* is created at the entrance, and it becomes larger and moves farther aft along the forebody toward the stern as boat speed increases. The narrower or finer the entrance and the longer the *waterline,* where the water meets the side of the boat, the less the bow wave's tendency to pile up and slow the boat. The length of the waterline is only partially a function of boat length. The length of the *overhangs,* the amount that a boat literally overhangs the water at bow and stern, is equally important. In some severe designs the waterline can be as little as half the overall boat length. Generally, the narrower boat will be the faster boat with a given amount of energy, and the longer boat will have a higher top speed.

The wider a boat is at its bilges amidships, corresponding with the beam in most boats, the stiffer and more stable the boat will be. This

Figure 3-1. General terminology for the parts of a kayak.

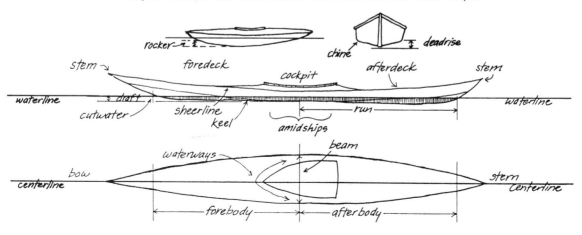

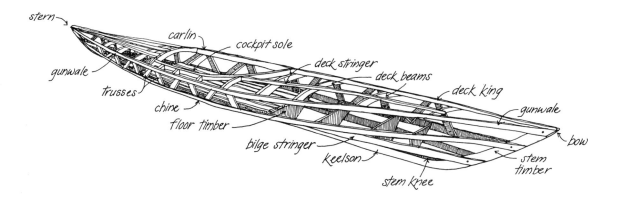

Figure 3-2. The construction members of a kayak frame.

makes sense if you consider that it is on the bilges or chines that a boat sits in the water, and on which the water pushes back when some force wants to tip over the boat. You can see that there can be a conflict of interest here. All boats are a compromise between being narrow for speed and wide for stiffness. To some degree a narrower boat may be made stiffer by having hard instead of soft bilges or chines. A soft-chine boat, such as a regular canoe, will feel very tippy and unstable when upright or at a low angle of heel. This is why beginning paddlers often feel insecure when they first board and attempt to use a canoe. But they soon discover that after the canoe heels over a way, perhaps as much as 30 degrees, the boat stiffens noticeably, and maintains this stiffness until it is tipped far over. The boat presents ever more bilge or chine on which it can respond with resisting buoyancy. A hard-chine boat places all of its potential buoyancy mass into the water right away, and so feels stiffer when upright or at low angles of heel. However, when a hard-chine boat heels way over, it is more likely to continue tipping and upset.

The rocker, the amount a keel bends upward toward the stems from amidships, also has an effect on boat performance. The more rocker a boat possesses, the less sideways resistance a keel presents to the water when the handler attempts to turn the boat. On the other hand, a long boat with little rocker will tend to resist turning, and so *track*—i.e., hold its course—better through the water. If you want to turn and maneuver easily and often, then have more rocker. If you wish to track steadily over long distances and not have your boat yaw and slough about with every paddle stroke, then have less rocker.

Our kayak is relatively long and narrow, with a hard chine, very little rocker, slight deadrise, and a very fine entrance.

The sides of a boat above the waterline are referred to as the topsides. *Gunwales* designate where the topsides meet the deck, and the profile of the gunwales when looking at the boat from the side is called the *sheer*. Following the sheerline along the outside of the gunwales is a strip of wood called the *rubrail,* in some places referred to as a *guard*. Amidships there is a large hole in the deck in which handlers and passengers sit. This is the *cockpit* and it divides the deck into the *foredeck* and *afterdeck*. Around the cockpit runs a thin sort of wall that rises above the deck surface and protects the paddler from deck wash. This is called the *coaming*.

THE FRAME

These general terms for parts of the hull are further embellished with terms for the construction members, the pieces of wood that compose the *frame* of the kayak. Harkening back to the materials that originally covered kayaks, we call the canvas or any other material that covers a kayak's frame the *skin*. Along the middle of the bottom are the *keelson* and *keel* of the boat, inside and outside the skin, respectively. At each end of the keelson, bow and stern, are *stem timbers* and these are reinforced onto the keelson with *stem knees*. At the chines are *chine strips,* and between the keelson and chine strips are *bottom stringers*. At the sheerline are *gunwale strips,* and between chines and gunwales is the trestlework, made up of *trusses*. At intervals all along the keelson, stringers, and chines are *floors* or *floor timbers* that lie athwartships. Similarly, at intervals athwartships from gunwale to gunwale are *deck beams,* which are tied together longitudinally by *deck stringers*. Around the cockpit and under or rather behind the coaming, are the *carlins*. These boats have no frames or ribs as do ordinary boat work or canoes.

All boats are built as they are so that any strain on one part of the boat is transmitted to, and so shared by, every other part. If the builder has in mind the purpose or function of a piece of wood as it is worked up and fitted into the framework, he or she will have a better understanding of why the piece is important and how best to fashion and fasten it, and so as to end up ultimately with a superior kayak.

The only parts of the framework to touch the skin are the longitudinal members, that is, the keelson, stem timbers, stringers, chines, gunwales, and deck stringers. This makes sense when you visualize what would happen if the athwartships members, the floors and deck beams, touched the canvas—there would be ridges going across the boat, making it slow in the water and ugly!

THE FORMS

The idea and purpose of the forms is to set up a stiff, rigid, temporary system of stations that will hold and lock the longitudinal strips in position to give the boat its shape while you fit and fasten the floors, trestling, and deck beams that tie the boat together. *Forms* is a collective term for six *stations* placed along a *centerline,* and two *uprights* that are used to hold up the stem timbers, placed at either end of the centerline. The whole is called the *setup.* The stations may be built of lumber, as prescribed in the 1923 Skene article (reproduced in full in Appendix A), but I suggest using plywood—at least ½-inch, preferably ⅝-inch plywood. Lengths of 2 × 4 stock work well for the uprights.

Neither the stations nor uprights become part of the final boat; they are used only in the first phases of construction, so the very cheapest plywood and 2 × 4 stock may be used. However, the manufacturing voids (holes and gaps) that exist throughout plywood and the warping, to which cheap wood of any kind is prone, can cause difficulties. An excellent compromise is to use the oiled exterior-type plywood that is used for cement foundation forms; this type generally has good-quality veneering, excellent gluing characteristics, no voids, and is relatively pleasant to work with. The American Plywood Association's designation for this material is "B-B Plyform, Exterior APA, PS 1–74." Whatever plywood you choose, you will need two 4-foot by 8-foot sheets of it.

This project does not require *lofting,* the laying down of the boat's lines full-size on a floor or wall, as does conventional boatbuilding. Rather, I have provided two tables of *offsets* (Figures 3–3 and 3–4), which you transfer directly to the plywood stock, thus establishing where to place the lines for sawing out the form stations.

The form stations establish the exact shape of the boat. The natural stiffness of the wood strips that go over and around the forms (keelson, bottom stringers, chine strips, and gunwale strips) and are temporarily attached to each station automatically creates fair, curving lines between the stations. If the stations are shaped and located properly, you will be able to see the shape of the kayak hull as soon as the seven strips are in place. All builders of boats, Old Salts and Boatshop Greenhorns alike, find such times in the birth of a boat very exciting and wonderful, for then internal visions are given hope of reality!

I provide two tables of offsets, one for a 17-foot kayak, and the other for an 18½-foot kayak that may be stretched to 21 feet simply by spacing the form stations and uprights farther apart.

The 17-foot kayak is ideal as a light, single-person craft used with a double-bladed paddle. Many two-person cockpit versions of this boat have been made, but such configurations should be reserved for protected and calm waters or for people interested in the more thrilling aspects of aquatic sport. The larger kayak is heavier, relatively wider, and large enough for a double cockpit that can carry two adults with camping gear and a small child, or accommodate a large adult with equipment, or take a sliding-seat rowing machine to be used with competition-style rowing (scull) oars. If you are using this book as your guide and instruction, you must choose one kayak or the other, and take your offset measurements from the table of offsets for that kayak. To avoid making a mistake, you may want to make a lightly penciled, cross-out mark through the set of offsets you do not wish to use.

The lines for each station are taken from the table of offsets and labeled A, B, C, and D. By the way, you might want to consider photocopying subsequent portions of this book, stage by stage in the construction process, rather than subject the whole volume to the vicissitudes of the workshop environment. Everything from here on is straight step-by-step instruction.

Making the Forms

Set up your sawhorses about six feet apart. Lay a sheet of your plywood lengthwise across the sawhorses.

Begin with the line B for station 1, as found in the table of offsets. Read that number, which is in inches and fractions of an inch, and locate that distance on your rule or yardstick. Open, take measure, and lock your dividers for this B measurement.

Set the point of the dividers on the bottom edge of a plywood sheet so that the pencil end comes inside the lower left-hand corner of the sheet. Mark the location of the compass point, then swing the compass, and tick off each end of the base thus established (Figure 3–6). You have now created the baseline B for this station; the mark at the point of the compass is the base of the station's centerline A.

To create the centerline A, erect a perpendicular line from the center point of B with a framesquare or T-square and lengthen this perpendicular line with a straightedge. This line must be precisely 90 degrees perpendicular to the baseline. Read the length of A for station 1 from the table of offsets. Locate this figure on your rule, and mark this distance on centerline A up from the middle of base B. You have now established the centerline and height of the station.

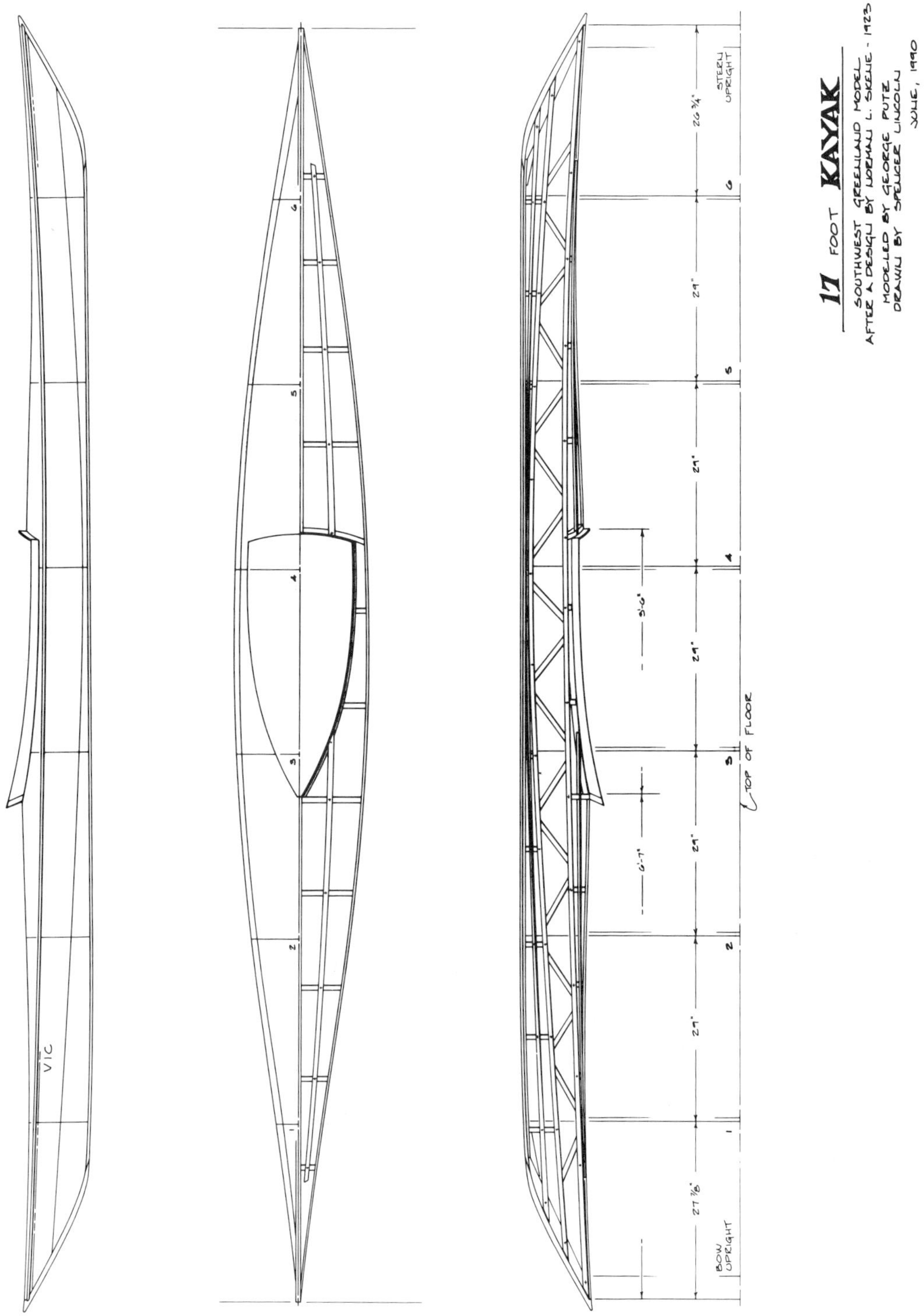
17 FOOT KAYAK
SOUTHWEST GREENLAND MODEL
AFTER A DESIGN BY NORMAN L. SKENE - 1923
MODELLED BY GEORGE PUTZ
DRAWN BY SPENCER LINCOLN
JUNE, 1990
STERN UPRIGHT
BOW UPRIGHT
TOP OF FLOOR

Figure 3-3. Lines for the 17-foot and 18 1/2-foot kayaks.

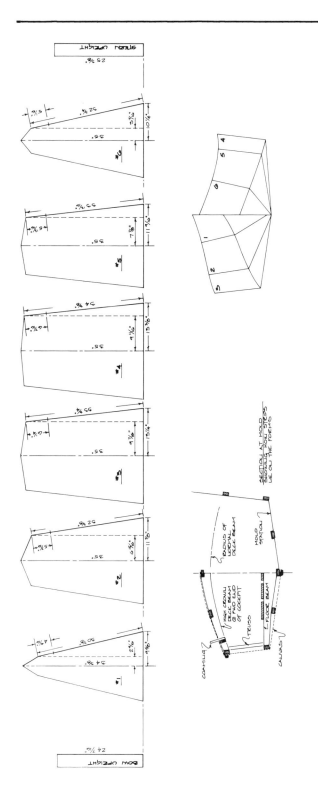

Figure 3-4. The table of offsets for the 17-foot kayak.

TABLE OF *OFFSETS*

SW GREENLAND MODEL AFTER SKENE 1923
17-FOOT VERSION

★ Distance from Bow Upright to #1 ...... 27 7/8"
★ Distance between forms .... 29"
★ Distance from Stern Upright to #6 .. 26 3/4"

	Bow Upright	#1	#2	#3	#4	#5	#6	Stern Upright
A	24 7/16"	34 3/8"	35"	35"	35"	35"	35"	25 5/16"
B		9 5/8"	11 7/8"	13 1/4"	13 3/8"	11 9/16"	10 1/4"	
C		2 7/16"	6 15/16"	9 1/16"	9 1/16"	7 7/8"	3 1/16"	
D		30 7/8"	32 3/8"	33 3/4"	34 3/8"	33 13/16"	32 3/4"	
E		26 9/16"	26 9/16"	27 1/2"	27 15/16"	28"	27 11/16"	
F		4 9/16"	5 1/16"	6 1/4"	6 7/8"	5 13/16"	5 1/16"	

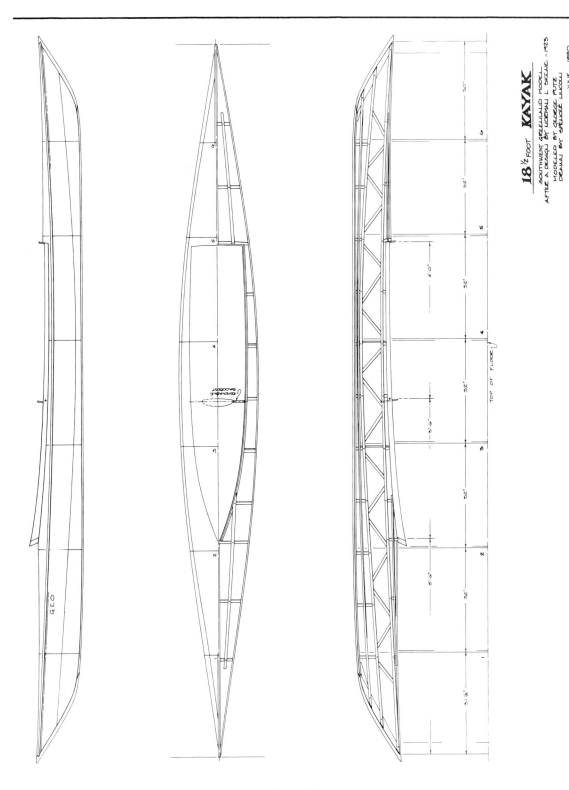

18½ FOOT **KAYAK**

SOUTHWEST GREENLAND MODEL
AFTER A DESIGN BY NORMAN L. SKENE - 1925
MODELED BY GEORGE PUTZ
DRAWN BY BRUCE LINCOLN
JUNE, 1980

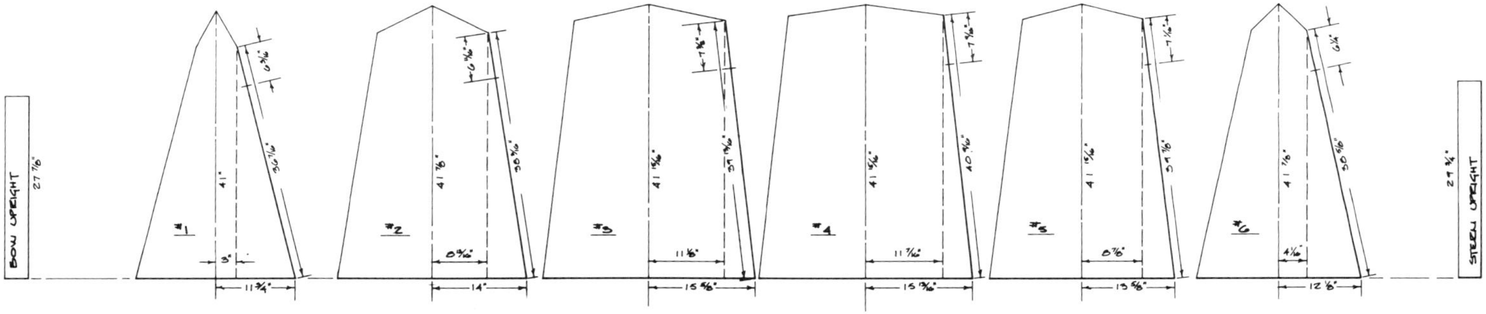

Figure 3-5. The table of offsets for the 18 ½-foot kayak.

TABLE OF OFFSETS

SW GREENLAND MODEL
AFTER SKENE 1923

★ Distance from Bow Upright to #1 .... 31⅛"
★ Distance between forms .... 32"
★ Distance from Stern Upright to #6 .. 30"

18½ FOOT VERSION

	Bow Upright	#1	#2	#3	#4	#5	#6	Stern Upright
A	27 7/8"	41"	41 7/8"	41 15/16"	41 15/16"	41 15/16"	41 7/8"	29 3/4"
B		11 3/4"	14"	15 5/8"	15 13/16"	13 5/8"	12 1/8"	
C		3"	8 13/16"	11 1/8"	11 7/16"	8 7/8"	4 1/16"	
D		36 7/16"	38 3/16"	39 13/16"	40 9/16"	39 7/8"	38 5/8"	
E		30 1/4"	31 8/16"	32 7/8"	33"	32 13/16"	32 3/8"	
F		6 3/16"	6 11/16"	7 3/8"	7 9/16"	7 1/16"	6 1/4"	

Figure 3-6. Swinging the dividers to establish "B" for form station 1.

Figure 3-7. Erecting a perpendicular to point "A" from the center of "B" for form station 1.

Be sure to double-check each of these measurements and points and to label them clearly.

With rule and dividers, set the dividers for C as read from the table of offsets for station 1. Set the point of the compass at the base of line A, which is also the center point of line B, swing the compass, and tick off the base points of the arc thus established. This creates the base points for the two perpendicular lines C. Erect two perpendicular lines C from these base points.

From the table of offsets, read the measurement D for station 1. Locate this measurement on your rule and mark it lightly, with a pencil. Place this marked rule so that the base, or zero, is at one end of baseline B, and the given distance just intersects the perpendicular line C on that side. Scribe the line, and then repeat this procedure on the other side. Note that the table of offsets includes measurements for E and F; these are subsets of line D. The point at which E and F meet establishes the gunwale strip placement and so determines the sheer of the craft.

Connect the tops of the C lines, thus established, with the top of centerline A.

You should now be able to see form station 1, laid out before you (Figure 3–8a).

Repeat these procedures for each station. You will conserve your plywood if you alternate back and forth from one side of the plywood sheet to the other, and draw out the forms in the order—1, 6, 2, 5, 3,

Figures 3-8A-C. Separating and sawing out the forms.

Wood and Canvas Kayak Building

A

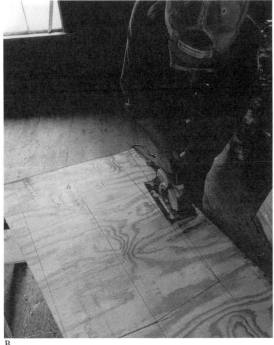

B

C

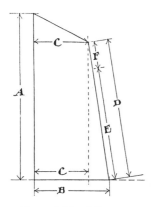

Figure 3-8D. Offset positions A, B, C, D, E, and F on a form station.

and 4. If you do this, you must concentrate on which form you are drawing, for your eye may easily slip from one column in the table of offsets to another. Try to keep at least an inch of waste space between each station. This allows them to be conveniently separated for individual treatment when you saw them out.

Sawing out the Forms

You should now be ready to saw out the forms. If you use a handsaw, be sure that it is sharp, finely set, and not too coarse to use on plywood. And may your shoulder and elbow survive the ordeal! If you use a powered circular handsaw, be sure that its blade is made for plywood and that you let the saw cool between sawing out each form. The set of plywood blades is very fine, and the work required of them is severe. Pacing and patience will prevent your saw blade and tool motor from burning out.

Saw close to your pencil lines but a tad to the outside so that the lines are entirely visible. Do not saw on the lines. Once the forms are sawn out, they need to be planed to their lines. Clamp them one at a time to a sawhorse, or chuck them by an edge into a bench vise, and use a finely set smoothing plane or block plane. Make light, short, side-slipping strokes to take out the high places. Then take one long, complete stroke so that you leave a perfectly straight edge, ideally leaving half the width

Figure 3-9. A sheet of plywood across the horses and entertaining the tools used in layout, minus the dividers.

Wood and Canvas Kayak Building

Figure 3-10. On the right are the set of forms we're making here for the 17-foot model. On the left are an older set of forms made for the larger kayaks, including the 18 ½-footer featured in this narrative.

of the pencil line still showing. Plywood is notoriously hard on tool steel, which is why some woodworkers prefer to keep a separate plane iron for work on plywood. If you have sharpened and honed your plane iron carefully and use a side-slipping stroke with the plane held at an angle to the stroke, chipping of the plywood edges and possible damage to the plane iron will be minimized.

Getting out the Strips

The completed form stations must be securely set up, aligned, and plumbed along a centerline struck on the work space floor. There are many ways to do this. Mine is perhaps a little elaborate, but justified because I reuse the forms, and a good alignment and bracing system prevents the damage caused by a wobbly setup.

To reinforce the forms I use 1-inch-square softwood stock ripped from scrap boards or plank stock; I fasten the pieces with screws across the station bases and alongside the centerlines A scribed on the forms (Figure 3–12). The vertical reinforcing piece must be off-center (just to one side of the centerline as scribed on the forms and as aligned on the floor) so that the mitered center braces may be located on-center yet be fastened securely to the reinforcing member and to the floor.

Plumbing and aligning the forms is worth considerable care and

Figure 3-11. Planing the forms to their lines. Eye-splicing demonstration in background courtesy of Edgar, also showing the importance of having onlooker's stools.

Figure 3-12. Bracing clamped to form station 2 and ready to be screwed into place.

effort. The correct shape of your kayak depends on it. First a centerline must be established on the floor, down the middle of your work space. This is most easily done with a carpenter's chalked snapline. Drive a small nail partway into the floor a foot or so beyond where you want the end of the boat to be. Hook the end eye of the snapline over this nail, and carefully pull the line taut along the floor in the exact direction you wish the boat to be oriented. Allow a foot or so extra length beyond where the other end of the boat will come. Stretch the line, hold it firmly to the floor, and give it one hardy snap. This establishes your centerline.

Along this centerline you must now mark with a pencil each location where a form is to be placed. These are your station marks, taken from the lines plans and offsets.

Reminder: If you wish to lengthen or shorten your kayak, now is the critical time to make the decision. Whether you are choosing to build the standard 17-foot model or the hardy 18 ½-footer makes no difference—the procedure is the same for both and very simple. Mark on the floor centerline where you want the ends of your boat to come and simply divide the overall length thus defined by 7, the resulting figure becoming the space intervals between stations. As a general rule, do not attempt to lengthen or shorten the smaller boat by more than a foot, nor the larger one by more than 1 ½ feet.

In any case, if you are building your kayak larger or smaller than shown in the lines, you must calculate your station spacing along the floor centerline so that it is proportional to the new size you have chosen. Station spacing must be strictly adhered to if the craft is to have a smooth, fair shape. Some leeway for spacing is allowed at the end uprights. The distance between the end uprights, on which the bow and stern stempieces set, and the station forms just in from the uprights may be varied somewhat according to taste. For example, if you want a very long, slicing bow, the distance between the bow upright and form station 1 can be increased a bit over what is called for in the plans. Or, if a more blunt, less pointy bow is wanted, the distances may be shortened a bit. The end uprights prescribed in the plans are the classic ones

Figure 3-13. Forms set up and aligned using pieces of shingle as shims. A keelson strip has been set into the centerline notches and used for sighting the alignment. Note clamps on the keelson at upper right where a scarf has been glued.

and I recommend them. You should now have the end points for bow and stern and each station clearly marked along the floor centerline.

Now strike bold, clear pencil lines 90 degrees to the floor centerline at each station mark, drawing these lines out so that they will extend the baselines of the station forms. These lines will be used to align the forms, and are best struck using a carpenter's framesquare that has been lined up with the centerline at each station and a straightedge to lengthen the lines thus established.

Before tacking the station forms into place, it will be useful and convenient to saw keelson notches into the apex of each form, as described near the end of this chapter. Longitudinal alignment of the craft is achieved by placing the keelson strip into these notches and sighting down the boat. It is easier to cut out the notches before the forms are set up, for it is the tacked-in-place keelson that will provide the initial rigidity to the setup along the top. Until the keelson is in place, the setup is generally wobbly, no matter how much reinforcement you use. Anyway, since we have now called for one of the structural strips, the keelson, we should discuss the keelson and other long members that go into the boat.

Longitudinal Members The keelson, stringers, chines, gunwales, and keel are all strips of wood that are the same dimension: In the case of the 17-footer they are ⅞ inch by ⅜ inch, and in the 18½-footer they are 1 inch by ½ inch. There are seven strips in all, one keelson, one keel, two bottom stringers, two chines, and two gunwale strips. They may all be of the same wood—spruce, cedar, or pine being the best choices—or you may wish to give the boat extra strength and use hardwood—oak or ash—for the keelson and keel. As I mentioned earlier, your best bet is to have your lumber supplier provide you with full-length finished-dimension strips, all cut out and planed. Next best is to get shorter lengths of dimension stock and scarf them into full lengths. If your local lumber outlets are unwilling or unable to provide you with finished-dimension strips, then you will have to provide them yourself from plank stock.

If such is the case, your plank stock should be finished (planed) as thick as your strips are to be wide—⅞ inch for the 17-footer and 1 inch for the 18½-footer. Make sure that the working edge of the plank is dead square, using your eye and a plane to make it so. If possible, try to use plank stock that is quartersawn (Figure 3–14), that is, comes from or near the center cut of the log and has grain that strikes across the thickness of the plank. Clear flitch- or slash-sawn plank stock will

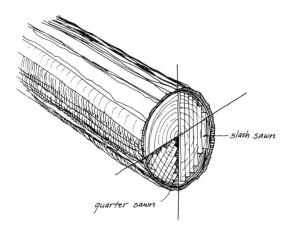

Figure 3-14. A quarter-sawn log. Quarter-sawn softwood is also called edge-grained, vertical-grained, or rift-sawed.

slash sawn

quarter sawn

serve, but the quartersawn stock is generally more stable, less prone to warpage, and gives a stronger yet more resilient boat.

Use a planer blade in your circular handsaw or table saw. This will give you a planed surface as you cut, saving you the tedious and difficult chore of planing long, thin strips of wood. Set the saw fence so that you will get the exact dimension cut you want (either 7/16 inch or 1/2 inch). If you have been fortunate enough to acquire full-length plank stock, cut out seven full-length, good, clear-as-possible strips. If your plank stock is not full length, 14 cuts will be necessary, so that you can scarf the strips to full length. Since this same dimension stripping will be necessary for deck stringers, the trestlework along the sides of the craft, and butt blocks to strengthen weak areas in the trestlework, make three or four extra cuts so that you will not have to go back to this arduous procedure later on. (By the way, should you begin to think that there is a lot of sawing in this kayak project, remember two things: First, there *is* a lot of sawing, at least at first; second, bear in mind that you are not scouring beaches of the Far North for pieces of driftwood out of which to individually split, whittle, carve, bend with teeth, and bind together with thongs the components of this kayak frame. Saw on, and think of paddling still waters.)

Scarfing   Strip scarfs should be at least seven-to-one (7:1), that is seven times as long as the stock is thick. Some older boatbuilders would say to double this, but modern epoxy glues are excellent, and if you make the scarfs fall where other screwed and glued members join, and so back the scarf, you can put your mind doubly at ease. In any case, the shorter scarf is easily made by eye, using a jackplane and smoothing the final surfaces with a smoothing plane on the two halves of the scarf set

The Parts of a Kayak   35

Figure 3-15. Snapping a chalkline on cedar plankstock in preparation for sawing out the strips.

Figure 3-16. A collection of strips, enough for two kayaks. Some have been scarfed where the clamps secure them while the glue cures.

side by side in a vise. Apply a modest amount of properly and well-mixed epoxy glue, set the pieces in place with finger pressure, scrape away excess glue with a splinter or toothpick, and clamp the work firmly but carefully between scrap pieces of strip stock (to prevent longitudinal slippage of the scarf). Repeat this procedure for all seven lengths of stripping. When the glue has hardened and cured, remove the clamps and pop apart the scrap pieces of wood. Lightly dress the scarf with medium-fine sandpaper to remove any burrwood or beads of glue.

Setting up the Forms   Whether sawn-out whole or scarfed, store your finished, full-length strips away from shop traffic. They are not convenient pieces of wood, do get underfoot if allowed, and are easily damaged or broken by the careless momentum of shop activity and visitors. Save one of the strips for the keelson, store the others out of harm's way, and let us return to the setting up of the forms.

Wood and Canvas Kayak Building

Using a short piece of scrap stripping as a template, notch the apex of each station form so that the keelson strip will just fit and be lightly held by the notch. Use the scrap strip to mark the location of the notch. Cut down both sides to the bottom line of the notch with a backsaw; cut across and just above the bottom line with a coping saw. Fair and fit the notch to the scrap piece of stripping with a small rasp or file. Do this for each station form.

We are now ready to set up. Lightly tack each form in its place, using the station lines and centerline on the floor as guides. Set the keelson strip into the apex notches, and sight down the strip to spot any gross problems in alignment. Tap the forms with a plastic, rubber, or wooden mallet to correct the alignment. Then use the framesquare or a small level to plumb the stations, and secure the stations with mitered station braces that have been cut from scrap rough lumber, as shown in Figure 3–17. Go back to the strip and sight down it, making corrections with shims (see Figure 3–13) as many times as is necessary to give a straight, fair boat. Wood shingles make excellent shims.

When the run of the keelson indicates that the boat is aligned laterally and vertically, go to each station, give it a final check for fore-and-aft plumbness, and then drill and nail the keelson to the form stations. These nails will have to be removed later on, so do not drive them all the way in. They are used at this point simply to hold the

Figure 3-17. Setting up form stations with mitered station braces. Note that stations 1 through 3 are braced to one side of the centerline; stations 4 through 6 to the other side of center.

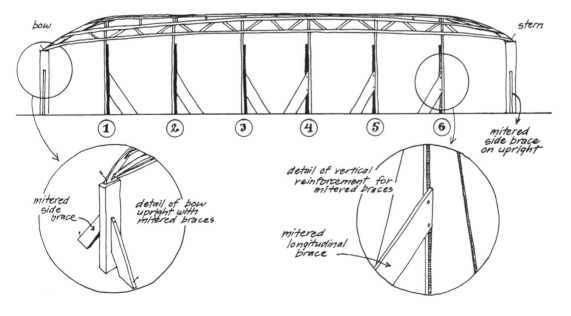

Setting up forms 1-6
with bracing details

bow

stern

① ② ③ ④ ⑤ ⑥

mitered
side brace
on upright

detail of vertical
reinforcement for
mitered braces

mitered
side
brace

detail of bow
upright with
mitered braces

mitered
longitudinal
brace

The Parts of a Kayak　　37

forms in vertical position and to tack the boat in its correct shape while other longitudinal strips are set into place. All the strips will be so nailed, the nails remaining in place until the hull frame is lifted from the forms.

At this stage, if the forms are aligned fairly, you can crouch down, sight along the run of the forms, and begin to see your future kayak. It is a most satisfying moment.

Uprights, Stems and Knees, Stringers and Chines

4

With your forms set up and keelson tacked in place, you are now ready to build the frame of the boat. Just as for the keelson, notches have to be let into the form stations for the bottom stringers. You can do this right now, or you can wait and insert these notches when you establish the stringers themselves. In any case, the stringer notches are created using the same procedure as for the keelson notches, with these two provisos:

- First, you do not cut down the vertical plane on the forms. Rather, you must cut from the perpendicular to the slant of the deadrise at each form station. This allows the canvas skin the full strip width against which to bear, rather than just one sharp edge of the strip.
- Second, at form stations 1 and 6 the angle of the deadrise is so severe that the notches must be relieved by cutting out the upper corners of the notches, so that the boat frame may be lifted off the forms after it is completed.

My own preference is to delay the creation of the notches until after the stems have been established, for then the whole system is tied together with the backbone of the boat (keelson, stems, and knees), providing some rigidity against which to do the sawing and rasping on the form stations. At this stage of the procedure there is still not much structure holding the system together, and things can come adrift. It is a matter of choice, and I mention it here instead of later simply because ordinary logic calls for completely developed forms before proceeding.

UPRIGHTS

Outside and at either end of the form setup you must establish uprights on which the ends of the stems will rest, affixed to the uprights by a temporary nail. As given in the table of offsets, the standard designated heights for these uprights are 24 $^{11}/_{16}$ inches at the bow and 25 $^{5}/_{16}$ inches at the stern for the 17-footer; 27 $^{7}/_{8}$ inches at the bow and 28 $^{5}/_{8}$ inches at the stern for the 18 $^{1}/_{2}$-footer.

This is, however, a place in the process where you may create some of your own design changes, provided you keep them within reason. Think about it.

Since the frame is being built upside down, it stands to reason that shorter uprights will give you a higher bow or stern. Conversely, higher uprights will render a relatively lower bow and stern. Keep in mind that our design provided here is modestly proportioned and time-proven. On the other hand, no two Eskimo kayaks were or are alike, and there is some space for discretionary changes at this stage. Remember that light watercraft are easily affected by wind, and that high ends catch the wind more easily than do low ends. Low ends, on the other hand, have less buoyancy and can make a boat "wet." Be judicious. Any reasonable adjustment here will not affect subsequent procedures.

For the uprights use stock that is at least 2 × 4, and saw it exactly to the given (or desired) height. Toenail it, centered precisely to the end mark of the chalked or scribed centerline on the shop floor (see Figure 4–5d). Ordinarily, the uprights are established in relation to stations 1 and 6 at the standard inter-station distance, depending on boat size. I use a toenail at each of the four sides of the upright stock; then, using a small level to plumb, I establish mitered side braces, made of ¾-inch scrap plank stock, from the sides of the uprights out to the shop floor (see Figure 4–5d).

It is time now to begin some of the most pleasurable woodworking in this project: getting out the stem timbers.

THE STEMS

In fabricating the stem timbers you have another opportunity to express your own preference and style in this craft. Indeed, it is in the profile of the bow and stern that a kayak takes on its special character, enough so that it deserves some discussion.

The proportions and offsets for Skene's original boat are provided in the plans, but only once in a dozen boats have I used them exactly.

Figure 4-2. Comparison of larger and smaller models, the latter an old boat and the subject of a later chapter. Note the difference in the sweep of the bows, a result of enlarging the forms almost 20 percent but spacing the forms out only 13 percent for the larger kayak.

Figure 4–2 shows the 18 ½-footer's bow next to that of a 17-footer built years ago, to which was added an outside dresspiece of oak that was scarfed to the keel. The 18 ½-footer's keel is simply bent up full-length, following in consistent dimension the profile of the stems and keelson inside the canvas skin. The stem timbers, remember, will be inside the skin covering, and while they do establish the basic profiles of the bow and stern, they need not necessarily be the last visual influence on them.

Whether you wish to stay with the original Skene stem profiles or not, it is a good idea to draft your stem-timber preference onto a piece of corrugated cardboard. Cut it out and hold the pattern thus created up to the proper location so that it intersects in profile the outside edge of the top of the appropriate (bow or stern) upright and presents a more or less fair curve into the keelson. At this point the keelson is extra long and hangs well past where it will be scarfed onto the stem timbers, but your mind's eye should be able to see the proposed curve and required scarf. Having built several of the rather straight, Skene-type bows in the past, I decided here to take a slightly different approach. I made a broad, sweeping pencil line on a piece of scrap plank stock, cut it out, and kept holding it up in position between upright and keelson (going back and forth between setup and workbench), touching it up with a smoothing plane until I achieved a pleasing profile. Since the 18 ½-footer shown here was being built with a rowing option, the

Figure 4-3. Using a piece of third-rate stock, I just cut out a sweeping curve pleasing to the eye, held it up to the upright and alongside the keelson strip to get roughly the required dimensions.

Wood and Canvas Kayak Building

Figures 4-4A-B. Once you have settled on a desired curve and determined the terminal points, trace the pattern onto the stock—in this instance an old bureau drawer front, here modeled by a vagrant working off a debt.

"rowboaty" profile was appropriate, but the results were good enough to carry over to the 17-footer. In both craft I used the stern stem-timber profile called for in the plans.

Go ahead and create your own special, personal bow and stern stem profiles, if you wish. You will have a beautiful, well-proportioned kayak, established in an authentic tradition, if you stick with the stem-timber profiles tendered in the plans.

Whatever your decision, the scarf between the stem timbers and keelson will come just outside the end form stations. On your pattern stock draw out the proposed lines, well beyond where they will terminate at the uprights and scarfs, cut out the pattern close to these lines, and dress to the lines with scissors (in the case of cardboard) or block plane (if you are using a more substantial pattern stock). Then, trace this pattern onto the construction stock, and cut it out using either bowsaw or band saw. Depending on your facility and tool preference, dress to the lines with small planes, rasps, or spokeshave. Touch-up sanding may be necessary, especially if you use rasps in your finish-shaping of these and all other components of the construction. Though my favorite tool for stems is the spokeshave, there is no right or correct tool here. I use them all according to problem and mood. A bit of sandpaper is never far away.

Stem stock can be of the same wood as the rest of the frame— indeed, the original plans called for it—but I usually choose a hardwood. Even though it adds a bit of weight, it is stronger and future users of the craft are given an extra margin of security in the event of collision and to mitigate the stresses often placed on kayaks during storage and transport. It is always the ends that bear the brunts. The stems of the boats pictured are made of oak taken from an old, discarded, bureau drawer-front. In the past I have used ash, apple tree limbs, and even spruce tree crooks (from where the tree expands at the ground) with perfect satisfaction.

Give the stem timber reasonable depth, 2 ½ to 3 inches, and make it exactly as thick as the keelson is wide, the whole tapering to beyond where you expect the scarf to come. Then hold the construction blank destined to become the finished stem up to the boat, from upright to a fair curve into the keelson, eyeball and steady it until it is just right, and then scribe a line from across the top of the upright onto the blank and another line onto the keelson where the line on the blank crosses it. When you make your cuts they will be final, so double-check every line!

Cut to the scribed line on the stem piece and fair it with a block or smoothing plane just as flat and perfectly as you can make it. Then set this flat surface onto the top of the upright and make sure that the

Figures 4-5A-C. Stems are sawn out and fitted to the upright and keelson, the latter usually cut off with a backsaw, but here with a crooked knife, an old Indian trade tool that still has a future. Note in 5B how the top corners of the stringer notches are relieved at the end stations to facilitate lifting the boat off the jig when the time comes.

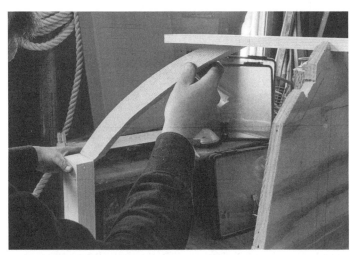

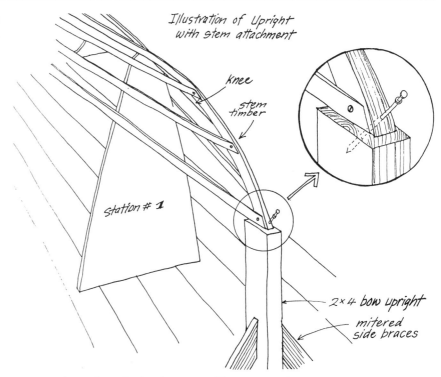

Figure 4-5D. Upright stem attachment. The stemhead is affixed to the top of the upright via predrilling a hole and toenailing in a double-headed nail. Note the mitered side bracing on the form.

Illustration of Upright with stem attachment

knee

stem timber

Station # 1

2×4 bow upright

mitered side braces

proposed scarf at the keelson is still coming where you expect it. Make whatever angle and fairing adjustments are necessary at the scarf end, and mark where the adjusting cuts on both stem timber and keelson are wanted. You will see now why it is best to begin with a cardboard pattern and a blank piece made larger than required before going through this drill with the actual construction stock, possibly several times before it comes right. Anyway, whether you have been chary with a pattern blank or bold with construction stock, finish your stem timber to shape.

Once you are satisfied that the stem is going to be OK, use the fine backsaw or dovetailing saw to cut off the waste keelson at the line, and dress it straight with a sharp block plane. Because of the relative thinness of the keelson, this dressing is not especially easy, so be sure to set your plane for very fine cuts and be gentle but firm, economical and careful. A short, positive, downward and side-slipping stroke with the plane will accomplish the task.

Finally adjust and dress the keelson/stem timber scarf surfaces. Remove any tatters that may remain on the tapered ends with a sharp knife or razor, perhaps leaving just a bit to be cleaned off after the glue in the scarf and knee joint has set and hardened. Knee joint? Yes. Clearly, the stem timber-to-keelson scarf is not large enough to be very strong, so a knee to back this joint is required for proper strength. You may, at this point, glue the scarf, but it is better to wait until the knees have been fabricated and fitted, gluing the whole together at once. A more reliable, easily dressed, better joint will result.

THE KNEES

The stem timber-to-keelson joints are obviously fragile and require the added strength provided by bow and stern stem knees. These are obtuse wedges of wood installed to thicken and reinforce these important joints.

The best way to determine the proper, inside-bearing angle of the stem knees is to enlist the services of an assistant, who holds the stem timber and keelson in relative position while you place the stock blank (soon to be the knee) against the setup and scribe the desired lines. Then get out the knee, refine it, and make the final fit right at the joint. As said above, I have found it best to complete both stem timbers, both keelson scarf surfaces, and both knees, gluing both ends at the same time with the same batch of adhesive. Since the resins have to harden at least overnight, this makes a good stopping place at the end of a productive day. You can regard your future craft with a completed backbone, the setup thoroughly tied together from end to end for the first time.

THE STRINGERS

This is a good time to make a final fairing of the setup. The tips of the stems should come to the middle of the top of the uprights and, when you sight down the length of the keelson, the keelson should make a straight, fair line along with the lateral and vertical axes. There should be no wobbles or curves from side to side, nor waviness up and down. Light taps with a rubber or plastic mallet against the side of the form stations will solve problems of lateral alignment. Shims, made of cedar shingle scrap, under portions of the form stations do just fine for the occasional height adjustments required.

Appearances are quite good enough on these boats. Absolutely dead true construction is neither practical nor necessary. The light trestle construction called for here is almost impossible to get perfectly fair, so do not be overly fussy. To a large degree these boats fair themselves as you go along, small imperfections canceling out one another. It is the accumulated errors that you want to avoid, but if you use and trust your eyes and work carefully and methodically, these will not be

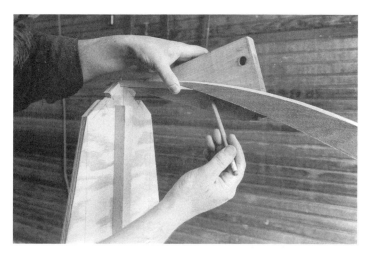

Figures 4-6A-B. Tracing the required knee onto stock and the assembly ready for gluing.

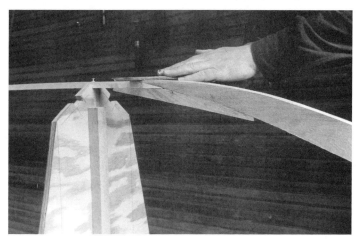

Figure 4-7. Rasping to true the glued-up joint.

introduced to the craft. Otherwise, it is the micro-variations from perfection that give all handiwork its special beauty, uniqueness, and vitality. Keep in mind that the entire framework will be covered with a canvas (or other appropriate) skin, which in turn will be dressed with exterior finish pieces. Small mistakes and repairs made along the way will be your secret.

If you have chosen to notch your forms for the bottom stringers after setting up the backbone (as I recommended), now is the time to let in the notches. This is done using the same procedure as for the keelson notches, except that the notches are trued to the bottom angle of each individual form, rather than to the vertical from the floor. Remember to use a short piece of strip stock to draw the notch lines on each form; then use the small backsaw, coping saw, and rasp to finish the notches. Note that notches go exactly midway between the keelson and the chines. Use a ruler to determine these centers on either side of each form, for a total of 12 notch locations. Notice that the bottom stringers destined for these notches will follow a sweeping curve, requiring that they be edge-set, that is, curved against their width, as well as their depth. This edge-set is not severe, however, and any appropriate wood stock will cooperate in the requirement. You can help the wood along, though, by visualizing the run of the curve that the stringers will have to take, and so aim the backsaw in the proper direction as you cut down into the forms. This will yield a snugger, friendlier notch system through which the bottom stringers will set. Finally remember that the framework eventually will have to be lifted off the forms and the bottom stringer notches at stations 1 and 6 will prevent this from happening. The upper corners of these notches will have to be removed later, a task made difficult by the nearness of the end floors to these form stations. If you want to avoid some close chisel work later, relieve (remove) these notch corners now, trusting to nail pins to hold the stringers in position.

Lay a full-length piece of strip stock into the notches along one side of the bottom, such that an equal amount protrudes at either end of the boat. Predrill holes and, using half-set, medium-small finish nails, pin the strip into the notches at form stations 3 and 4. Then place a Vise-Grips pliers over two pieces of squared wood scrap and onto the stringer about five inches inside of where the strip must be scarfed to the stem timber. This scarf's location may vary—let the wood tell you—but it is usually at or just above the stem knee. Using the Vise-Grips as a handle, give the stringer end a firm twist and observe closely how the scarf should go along the strip in order for it to join with the stem timber. The first time—and maybe other times—you will want to just eyeball the scarf placement, to practice looking at the pieces involved, perhaps lightly drawing your proposed cut for the scarfing surface. When you are confident, you then must make the cut, for which there is a choice of tools.

In boatbuilding practice the tools generally used for this type of cut through this sort of stock are the boatslick and the boat spud; both are very large, relatively rare chisels, requiring practice in their use. They make quick work of such cuts. Ordinary, handy mortals must settle for a large, sharp knife, the largest finish chisel you own, or my favorite tool, the North American Indian crooked knife. (These knives are still inexpensively available from the North West Company, believe it or not! See Appendix B.) In any case, if at all possible, make the cut in one firm push or pull of the tool, out just a bit from where the final surface is wanted. Then, holding the torqued strip out from the stem timber, keep lightly dressing the scarf surface with a block plane until you have a fair fit. Once your initial orienting cut has been made, you can relieve the twist and get the waste off without strain. Finishing the surface, though, must be done by twisting the strip and getting the side of the stem timber and the scarf surface to face perfectly.

Keep this in mind: Since there is no exactly right or correct fall for these scarf joints at the stems, the first bottom stringer that you mount is relatively easy. However, when you begin to establish the second stringer on the other side, it has to be as nearly symmetrical as possible with the first one. So, relatively more care and precision has to be exercised on the second side than on the first, this duty made somewhat easier by the fact that you have practiced on two previous joints.

Once satisfied that the fit will be good, predrill and slightly countersink holes for the retainer screws that will hold the joint tight while the glue sets. Use a drill bit of the same wire size as the fastener—bronze ⅜-inch #6 for the 17-footer, ⅝-inch #7 for the 18½-footer. Also predrill holes for nail pins at the remaining unpinned stations, and place finish nails in them, ready to fix the stringer strip firmly in the notches. Mix a batch of glue, apply it to the scarfing surface of the strip, place the surface in position, screw it, clamp it, and pin it. Use any good, modern, waterproof adhesive. On these boats I use regular, hardware-store, clear epoxy, the type that comes in a two-part syringe. Many craftsmen will criticize this choice, saying that such glue contains fillers and is very expensive by volume. My answer is that the volume used in this project is small, the adhesive characteristics are very adequate, and the dispensing system is precise and neat.

Do not worry about glue drips or a little overhang, or slightly imperfect symmetry of the scarf on the other side of the stem timber.

These all can be scraped and sanded fair after the glue sets and hardens. Note, however, that any large knobs or unfair protuberances, in addition to being unsightly, will show through the canvas skin later on, providing places where chafing can occur, and so leaks. Also, since these scarfs are long and thin, the wood near the end may not be able to take the whole head of the screw, in which case back the screws out and leave them out after the glue hardens. Any screw heads that stand proud inevitably will cut through the canvas skin that covers them.

Both ends of both stringers need to be affixed to the stem timbers in the above fashion.

Figures 4-8A-D. Roughing, planing, fitting, and installing the first bottom stringer. Note Vise-Grips used to torque stringer into position.

THE CHINES

The chines constitute the outside lines of the bottom of the boat. If everything has been done properly in shaping and installing the form stations, the chine strips should make fair curving lines along the outside of the upper corners of the forms stations. The design of the forms is such that the chine strips need no notches to hold them in position (see Figure 4–9). By predrilling holes and using finish nails, chine strips are pinned along the outside of the form stations, right at the corner edges, and then scarfed into the stems at either end and both sides, just as were the stringers. You will find that the chines are much easier to install than the bottom stringers, for only a slight twist is required to achieve proper alignment with the stem timber's surface.

Chine strips should fair into the stem timbers anywhere between one-third and one-half the distance up the stems toward the top where the stems rest on the uprights. Scarf, glue, screw, and finish pinning the chines, just as you did for the bottom stringers.

You may now proceed directly to the installation of the floor timbers.

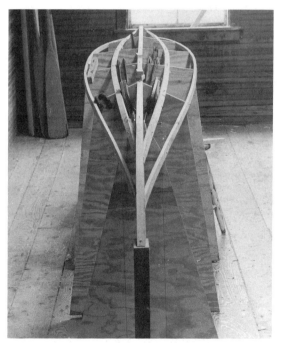

Figure 4-9. Stringers and chines in place.

Figure 4-10. Detail of stringers and chines at the stem-timber. Note the liberties taken with the fairing of the stringers (upper strips in the photo). It's OK. A little fairing off and she'll look just fine.

Floors, Gunwales, Trestlework, and Deck Beams

5

THE FLOORS

You have installed five strips of wood—the keelson, two bottom stringers, and two chines—into the stem timbers. These now need to be tied together, down the entire length of the boat. You do this with floor timbers, which we will call simply floors. In fabricating the floors you again get to do a bit of boatbuilding as the term is ordinarily applied to occidental watercraft. Each floor is custom fabricated and fitted to each strip. Getting out the rough piece for each floor, and then making it fit well at all five bearing places involves much walking back and forth between setup and workbench. Be careful and methodical in the work, and do not become discouraged if your first attempt is not successful. The biggest hazard is to take off too much wood in the shaping process. So, be conservative. It is much easier to return to the bench to remove more wood, than it is to try to replace what has been removed. Don't worry if you botch it; just start afresh to make the piece. The pieces of wood involved are small and easily replaced and worked. The learning curve is steep but cheap for a good job.

Floors are located at each station and halfway between stations. I like to place them on the front of each form station, toward the bow, but it is inconsequential whether you choose the forward or after side of the stations for floor placement. Eleven floors need to go into the craft at regular intervals, and mounting six of them directly against the form stations assures that at least that many will be perfectly aligned athwartships, 90 degrees to the keelson. The others, which come between the stations, are located by measurement and eye, sometimes with a bit of fore-and-aft fudging. The important thing is that your floor timbers remain true to the fair curve of the strips they tie together, and that they in fact do tie them together!

Use the same stock for the floors as you used for the strips, the same thickness as the strips. Make the floors' bearing surfaces as wide as the strips (see Figure 5–3). The first and most difficult floors to be installed are those at either end of the craft.

Approach the craft from either form station 1 or 6 with a rule in hand and measure the distance between the insides of the two chine strips; write it down. Then, using a straightedge, measure the distance at that station from the tops of the chines to the top of the keelson; write it down. Remember that, since the boat is being built upside down, top and bottom are reversed as absolute designations. Both chine and keelson tops are the surfaces closest to the shop floor.

Use these measurements, allowing a little extra wood, to cut out your end floor blanks from plank stock. Then take the blank in hand and hold it up in the desired position. With a pencil make light, conservative marks where wood should be removed to make a good fit. Several fittings may be required, for, except at the keelson, the bevels at stringers and chines are double bevels, with slants in two planes. The back-and-forth between setup and bench that this entails is tedious but worth it. You will discover that by the time you have reached the other end of the boat, you are a floor expert.

Because they are shallower from top to bottom, the other floors,

Figure 5-1. Roughing out the first floor timber on either the stock itself or a piece of cardboard is acceptable practice. Be prepared for a disappointment or two right here; however, things soon improve.

Wood and Canvas Kayak Building

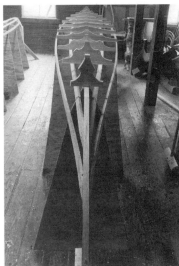

Figures 5-2A-B. Finished, fitted floors ready for gluing.

numbers 2 through 10, are much easier to make and fit than the two end ones.

At each location, measure the distance between the chines, and transfer this measure to blank stock, cutting the stock squarely. On this floor blank, draw a baseline and erect a perpendicular line from the center of the baseline. Hold the floor blank centered under the chines and look down through the strips; you should be able to see the need for the double bevels, canted down on the after part and sideways. By eyeball trace the required bevels. Keep in mind that the floors toward the ends require ever-increasing double bevels. Then sight in the articulation points, where the strips will bear on the floors, and tick these off onto the blank with a pencil. Rough out the blank for close-fitting. The creation of floors is a tailoring process; each floor is custom-fitted. The process is time-consuming and, especially if you attempt to hurry or make shortcuts, emotionally trying. Since floors must reflect each craft's idiosyncrasies no photograph or illustration will answer every question; so, study the pictures here, study your frame, and put yourself in a mind to enjoy the meditative tailoring process.

Once the articulation surfaces of each floor have been created and fitted, I like to saw and rasp out a semicircle of waste wood between them, making each bearing surface distinct, and also saving a bit of weight in the boat. For the little extra work involved, it makes the frame look terrific.

Follow the procedure for each floor, at each floor location.

Figure 5-3. Installing floor 2.

I like to get out all of the floors prior to installing them. A look at Figures 5–2a and 5–2b may show why. Whether that way, or one at a time, each needs to be sited, glued, and screwed into position. Having marked on the strips exactly where the floors fall, set up a systematic installation procedure. I like to mix small amounts of glue, enough for two floors at a time. Then, on a low stool I place an electric drill with countersink bit, a box of screws (same size as mentioned above for the stringer and chine ends), and a glue-application paddle, which is usually just a piece of whittled scrap wood.

Here is my procedure: Take a floor in hand, hold it in position with one hand, and with the other hand drill holes at chine, stringer, and keelson. Then go to the other side and drill the opposing stringer and chine. Remove the floor from position, spread glue on the five articulation surfaces, reposition the floor, and fasten it into place with screws. Scrape away any obvious glue drips.

I'm not sure how much walking is involved in getting out the floors, going back and forth between setup and bench, one side of the boat to the other. It is at least a few miles, but you smell wood, not "PDQ4-Polyvinylethylmethylketonegoddamnerate-11," while you work, even though there is a smidgen of something similar in your glue.

Wood and Canvas Kayak Building

THE GUNWALES

In establishing the gunwales, the upper outside edges of the boat where topsides and deck meet, you have another opportunity to customize your kayak—to make it distinctively your own craft, without changing the procedures called for in this book. If you wish, now is a time for some creative fun.

Clearly, the ends of the gunwale strips must come down to where the stem timbers sit on top of the uprights. But the sheerline, or how they run fore-and-aft between the stems, is up to you. Within limits, you may fix the sheerline wherever you want it. Since the boat is upside-down, an aspect with which the eye is not always comfortable, you may want to regard the sheerline-fixing process by looking at the boat with your head either down between your legs or off to the side of either thigh. In any case, you will derive a fine-looking kayak if you stay with the sheerline placement as given in your table of offsets.

On the form stations, tick off with a pencil the locations of the tops of the gunwale strips, as called for in the table of offsets. Drive a medium-size finishing nail partway into the sides of the forms at each tick mark. Then, take a strip of wood and, resting it on the form

Figure 5-4. A gunwale strip resting on a line of nails. Here is yet another place where you can be your own designer.

stations' line of nails, lightly pin the strip against the side of the stemheads and set it on the uprights. This procedure will show you the sheerline as designed.

If you are pleased with this sheerline (it is classic and wonderful), go with it! The slightly unfair places, where the nails come a little bit too high or low, are easily corrected. When you have adjusted the gunwale strip so that it is fair from end to end, predrill and pin the strip at the stations 2 through 5; sight, cut, and let in the gunwales to the stem timbers, following the standard procedures as established for the other strips. Make the gunwale strip's end apexes come exactly to the point of the stemhead.

If you have opted to use the sheerline called for in the plans, ignore the next paragraph.

To create your own custom sheerline, do this: Look at the sheerline with your head down, inverted on the perpendicular (to one side of either thigh) or, if you can manage it, regard the setup with your head upside down between your legs. From one of these positions, you can see the proposed profile of the rightside-up craft. Use your imagination. Among the reasons for possibly changing the sheerline are—

- First, special physical requirements of the person or persons who will use the boat. Especially large or small people should be considered, and their needs may call for changes in the usual form of the craft. If two people, of any sort, will share the cockpit, this may also be taken into account.
- Second, special conditions of climate, weather, or sea conditions for which the kayak is intended or destined may require a sheerline configuration that differs from the standard one provided.
- Third, special uses for which the boat is intended may call for changes in the sheerline. People who want to hunt aquatic birds from their craft or to cartop their boat may want a lower, flatter sheerline. Family boats meant for picnics, cargo, and optional crew will want a higher sheerline. Paddlers who want speed and efficiency in their kayak may want to lower the profile of the boat.

Bear in mind that the sheerline option offered here is complemented by a deck-camber option later on, which allows some of the same advantages of choice, only for the deck-centerline profile. By lowering or raising the run of the gunwale strip, you can make whatever changes you want, within reason.

Measure the distance from the shop floor to the new nail-stop positions at each form station on the regarded side. Duplicate the nail-stop positions on the opposite side, and then repeat the installation procedures for the gunwale on that side. Drill and pin the gunwale strips into position. Then, drill, glue, and screw the scarf-surfaced ends into the heads of the stems, as previously described for these and the other longitudinal strips.

THE TRESTLEWORK

The frame's side strength is provided by trestlework between the chines and gunwale strips (see Figures 5–6a and b and Figure 3–2). The pieces of trestling are installed between the form stations, and, while they are critical to the overall strength of the structure, they need not be fine work. Perfect shaping and positioning of the individual pieces is not necessary, for none of them bear on the outside shape of the boat. However, don't let this proviso get in the way of a careful job; there are many pieces involved and the tedium of fabricating and installing them encourages a rush job. When fitting and fastening these pieces, keep in mind what the trestlework has to do on the water over the next (at least) 10 years.

The chines have some twist in them toward the ends of the boat, therefore some inletting of the top members of the trestle is necessary in these areas. The stock used is of the same type and dimension as for the strips; indeed, the scrap ends of the strips are ideal for this purpose, and nearly enough for the work—another reason why extra strips were recommended in Chapter 2.

Mark off each form-station interval into thirds. Break or cut off a

Figures 5-5A-B. Two photographs showing not only the articulation of stringers, chines, trestling, and floors, but the use of butt blocking at weak places and the placement of scarfs so that they are through-screwed for added safety.

Figures 5-6A-B. The finished framework. Note the trestling. Details of the cockpit framing are described in Chapter 6. PHOTOS BY RICK STAFFORD.

blank piece of wood from strip stock and hold it into position between an end form (station 1 or 6) and the first (one-third) distance mark. Scribe the cutting lines above the chine and below the gunwale; cut the piece to these lines. Then eyeball how much, if any, the piece needs to be let in for a good fit. Where fitting is necessary, use a rasp to let. Be conservative and make a couple of trips to the bench to fit. Then drill, glue, and screw the trestle piece into position.

As with the floors, several pieces can be got out and prepared before installation. There is much glue-mixing, drilling, and fastening activity during this stage. But the purpose and process is utterly straightforward. Look at the trestlework in the structural drawing (Figures 3–2 and 3–5), and then duplicate its appearance, purpose, and effect in the shop. There is a pleasant rhythm in trestling. It goes quickly. And when it's done you can really see how the boat will appear, even though it is upside down on the forms!

Indeed, if you want, you can remove the boat from the forms now and play with it, albeit gently and only for a little while. Some would caution against the temptation, for without the deck beams in place the boat lacks lateral strength; but this weakness is not so severe that a bit of pride and hands-on planning cannot be indulged. To remove the frame first carefully remove all of the pinning nails. Be sure that the stringer notches at form-stations 1 and 6 are relieved to allow upward removal of the craft from the forms. Be gentle, and do not leave the boat off of the forms more than a couple of hours. Once indulged, carefully reposition the boat frame back onto the forms. No repinning should be necessary, nor any reminder that this project is immanently worthwhile.

THE DECK BEAMS

You now want to establish the same strength across the top of the boat with deck beams, as you did earlier across the bottom of the boat with floor timbers. The deck beams are of the same stock used for strips and floors, with two exceptions. The deck beams mounted at either end of the cockpit should be manufactured a bit stouter, either by increased

width dimension with the usual stock, or to width dimension with stronger hardwood stock.

Again, here you have an opportunity to customize the nature and character of your boat by deciding how much camber you want for the deck; that is, how much elevated crown or curvature you want upward from a straight horizontal line erstwhile cast straight across opposing gunwales. Many of the native craft of this type had laterally flat decks. Most modern American kayakers like a good deal of camber, for it gives more internal space, more residual buoyancy, and sloughs off seas and spray quickly and efficiently. On the other hand, duck-hunters and cartoppers like low profiles. In any case, you need to make a pattern here, and this is simply a matter of striking a cord of a circle—a relatively small circle for a high camber, a relatively large one for a low camber—using a pencil, a length of string, and a piece of corrugated cardboard on which to strike a cord of a circle broad enough to span the boat at its beam width.

Using a length of string as a radius—between 2 feet and 2 feet 9 inches respectively, for relatively high and low deck camber profiles (these measurements hold true for both long and short models), pin one end of the string with your thumb to the shop floor or the top of the workbench, so that a pencil affixed to the other end of the string at your prescribed length will scribe a semicircle across the cardboard. Then draw the cord between outermost terminals of the circle segment and erect a perpendicular from the halfway point of the cord. Cut out the semicircle and finish it to the line so that a pencil tracing the pattern onto deck beam stock will strike a fair curve. You are now armed to get out the deck beams.

As with the floor timbers, you here must face some walking back and forth between setup and workbench, but it is not nearly so tiresome because, first, there are fewer deck beams than floors and, second, the deck beams have only two articulation points (the gunwales) rather than five. Keep in mind the uses and abuses to which your boat will be put, and the fact that deck stringers will be installed down the length of the deck, across the deck beams, as you determine what width to make the deck beams.

Deck beams need to be installed at regular intervals out to the ends, both forward and aft of the cockpit. Deck beam stock may be of the same wood as used for the floors and strips. Using the lines plan (Figure 3–5) as a guide, locate and mark along the gunwales where the deck beams should be located. This can be a rough designation. An inch or two forward or aft of the designed location is of no consequence. The function of these members is to maintain lateral shape and strength,

Wood and Canvas Kayak Building

and to provide articulation points for the deck stringers, on which the deck canvas will bear.

Beginning at either end of the boat, cut out a piece of stock to the width between the insides of the gunwales at the first designated location, leaving some extra. Scribe a straight line across the intended bottom of the stock blank. Or just use one edge of the stock, if you have some that is straight. Then, being conservative and by eyeball, cut, rasp, and fit the bottom of the blank stock into position between the gunwales. *Remember that the bottom of the deck beam blank is uppermost as you regard the blank—you are installing these members upside down.* When you have achieved a fit, mark where the tops of the gunwales intersect the blank. Then take the cardboard-and-cord pattern you have created and align it such that the circle pattern connects the upper gunwale edge marks on the deck beam blank. Scribe the circle from mark to mark, and cut out this circle to the line with bowsaw or band saw, finishing with spokeshave (or small plane), rasp, and sandpaper. Measure across the bottom of the blank stock and mark the halfway point. From there, using a bench square, erect a perpendicular, scribing it in pencil. This gives both an absolute and visual centering line for you to use in properly aligning the deck beam. If you want to save weight in the finished craft, re-scribe the circle cord well inside the outer perimeter of the beam, allowing enough wood for adequate strength of the member (at least 1 ½ inches), and cut away the waste wood, finishing the new surface with rasp and sandpaper.

Predrill and countersink screw holes; glue and screw the beam into position. Follow this procedure in shaping and installing four beams into the foredeck and three beams into the afterdeck of the boat, leaving a relatively large space amidships for determination and fabrication of the cockpit size, layout, and construction.

The Cockpit Deck Beams

You must now establish your cockpit location, shape, and dimensions, and here again you have considerable latitude in discretion and choice. How large to make your cockpit, in both length and width, and exactly where to locate it, is a matter of who will use the kayak, where, for what purposes, and with what gear or equipment. A smooth-water boat for two people and a big picnic basket calls for a large open cockpit. A single sportsperson intending to go into harm's way and perform Eskimo rolls in a seaway will want a cockpit into which there is barely room to squeeze.

Figures 5-7A-B. Note the deck camber on this finished frame is higher forward and has a more elevated crown than does the after cockpit frame. PHOTOS BY RICK STAFFORD.

A safe bet is to go with the plans as designed and shown. In practice I locate the proposed center of user weight, usually about three-fifths (³⁄₅) of the distance abaft the bow for large-cockpit boats, and slightly forward of this for small-cockpit boats. It is useful to pop the framework off the forms, have someone (preferably the person who will most often use the craft) sit down into the framework, and determine by sight where on the gunwales to mark the forward and after ends of the cockpit, where the cockpit deck beams will go. Such appearances are reliable, for what looks good is good, in this case.

At any rate, the deck beams at the ends of the cockpit need special consideration. They should be a bit heftier than the others, either by increasing the dimensions applied to the regular wood stock, or by making them out of hardwood to the usual dimension width. The aft cockpit deck beam should have a bit more camber than the others, and the forward deck beam should be given a boomerang shape, an obtuse V-shape. This lofty triangular section allows more thigh room, facilitates getting in and out of the craft, and allows the forebody deck stringers to be faired into the cockpit construction with ease, and to better appearance. This said you will notice in the photographs of the larger kayak that this was not done, the greater size of the boat and its rowing option making it unnecessary and undesirable. The high peak of the cockpit as originally designed would present a hazard to the back of a rower using a sliding seat. The design drawing (Skene's lines)

displays the proper boomerang shape of this forward cockpit deck beam member.

Figure 5-8. Lots of latitude for cockpit size and shape!

Another possible customizing option to consider is whether to give the aft cockpit deck beam a double curve in two planes; not only a camber, but also a chairback curve on the longitudinal axis. Such a crafting and installation makes leaning back in the finished cockpit more comfortable, and adds a touch of class. For good stock in this application I have often used a curved branch from an elderly fruit tree pruning, but in the photographs here the stock came from a discarded, red oak chairback, which had a thickness and width that allowed adequate dimensions—curvature and camber—for the purpose.

Site, shape, finish, and install the forward and after cockpit deck beams, using the procedures described above for the other deck beams.

FREEING THE FRAME AND PREPPING FOR CANVASING

The forms have done their duty now. Remove the boat frame from the forms, and set it aside. Carefully dismantle the form-station support members by prying the system apart, removing all nails. Then gather and store the form stations in a dry, safe environment for possible later use.

Although in the original article Skene proposed that the bottom canvas should be dressed onto the frame bottom before the boat is removed from the forms, I have found that the use of modern epoxies reduces the likelihood of the boat changing shape when displaced from the forms. Skene properly feared this because of his day's reliance on simple double-screwing and no use of adhesives whatsoever. Using the methods and techniques I propose and describe, there are no problems and considerable advantages in being able to move the boat around, working on it stretched between sawhorses, wherever and at whatever angle you wish.

Nevertheless it is a good idea to apply the bottom canvas before installing the deck stringers. The boat can then rest firmly on the gunwales rather than wobble back and forth on the deck stringers while the canvas is being applied.

Set the kayak framework onto sawhorses such that the sawhorses come between deck beams and support the boat on its gunwales. Now is the time for double-checks and cosmetic refinement of the bottom framework. Any potentially weak places in the framework should be sistered (butt-blocked) by gluing lengths of scrap strip stock inside suspect areas—i.e., any knots, hooks, saplines, or checks that you have permitted in the structure. (See Figures 5–5a and 5–5b for an illustration of butt-blocking.) Any dents, dings, or holes in the wood should be filled and faired using plastic wood compound. Too, it is a good idea to go over the entire form with a light sanding. Use a sanding block and medium-grit sandpaper, especially along the edges of the stem timbers and chines where the canvas skin has to wrap around severe corners, and so will be prone to chafing. Any and all protuberances and burr areas also should be sanded fair and smooth. Use your eyes and hands; look at and feel the framework from every angle and aspect.

Finally, in cases where the frame is made of pine or spruce (or other vulnerable wood), a good coating of oil does not hurt, and probably helps the longevity of the craft. Clear Cuprinol is OK, but I prefer a simple 1–1–1 mix of linseed oil, turpentine, and kerosene, to which I add three tablespoons of ordinary fungicide, the type available at most hardware stores.

For better or worse, your boat is now an independently free object in the world. Imagination is not needed to see its form. You enter the middle stretch of the construction process as you contemplate application of the bottom canvas skin.

Bottom Canvas, Cockpit Carlins, Deck Stringers, Deck Canvas, and Painting

6

The idea that your brand-new kayak frame is now an independent object in the world is exciting, to be sure, but it also presents you with some problems. What you have in effect is a rigid, light, intriguingly shaped, trestleworked hull frame that is now subject to hazards from which its marriage to the forms previously protected it. In its loose, independent state it is much more subject to damage, not only because it is an attractive object that people want to touch, but because its unattached character makes it prone to accident during the remainder of the construction process.

There are two effective things that you can do to protect your new kayak frame. First, announce and enforce a no-touch policy among your intimates and friends. Assure them that the day will soon come when they all can paddle and enjoy the boat, but that meantime they are not to touch it—or even slightly heft an end of it without permission and your own good offices.

Second, since the balance of your work on the boat will be across sawhorses (or their equivalent), it is a good idea to cushion the sawhorse tops with carpet remnants. Upholstery and carpet outlets often have such scraps or product samples of no use to them; the same is true of interior decorating firms. Pick out a scrap or sample large enough to cover the tops of two sawhorses, with enough remainder to come over the sides and present a good tacking or stapling surface. A few minutes dressing these work surfaces will prevent dings and nicks in the framework as you canvas the bottom, on the bottom canvas as you finish out the deck, and altogether as you go through the procedures of finishing the boat. Canvasing, especially, involves a lot of pulling, jerking, and hammering (tacks through the canvas into the gunwale strips), and this protective measure allows you to do it all with more effect and in good conscience.

CANVASING THE BOTTOM

It has been my purpose in this book to offer as many choices as possible; optional ways of conceiving and executing procedures in the project. This kayak design lends itself to this sort of creativity, giving no harm and allowing you to build a craft that is more yours than mine or this book's. Here, as has become the habit of this book, you again have a choice. You can canvas the bottom now, which I recommend, or you can proceed to the following subsections of this chapter and finish framing the deck before you canvas the entire craft at one time. I suggest canvasing the bottom before framing the deck because the deck as finished has a camber (an athwartships curving hump), which, if framed to specification, will cause the boat to rock back and forth on the deck stringers—very inconvenient and irksome while you attempt to stretch and tack the bottom canvas in place. On the other hand, the suggested bottom-first priority has its own drawback. Framing the deck on the upright craft, over the canvased bottom, involves all kinds of woodworking that will rain chips and sawdust down into the bilges, trapping this effluvia between the wood strips and canvas skin. So, the tradeoff is a more stable boat on which to apply the bottom canvas versus an assiduous sweeping and vacuuming before applying the deck canvas. It's up to you. I stick with early bottom-canvasing.

My final proviso here is to say that there are optional ways to skin this kayak. Both carbon-fiber-reinforced Kevlar and heat-shrunk, aircraft Dacron offer very acceptable alternative ways to cover this frame. These contemporary high-tech options offer lighter and in some ways tougher boats. If you want to consider these optional skins, the materials manufacturers will help you choose the correct fabrics and chemistries. Follow their recommendations carefully. I point this out because it makes no difference what skinning technology you use. The procedure is the same for all boat coverings. Because we have chosen a traditional approach in the construction of our craft, we are going to select the skin material in the same vein. We will elect to use the traditional canvas, cotton duck. You are, of course, free to choose an acrylic or other synthetic cloth. We are going to canvas this boat.

Cotton (duck) canvas is not so common or easy to find as it once was. Nearly every nautical use it once enjoyed—sails, deck coverings, mast coats, and even clothing—has shifted almost entirely to synthetic fabrics. Very few marine chandleries or sailmakers still carry the product. If you live near to a large chandler or sail loft that services traditional boatyards, certainly approach it first. But most people in most places will have better luck by contacting a local firm that makes custom awnings. While it is not likely to have 10-ounce, 4-foot-wide canvas in stock, the firm's regular suppliers will, and the canvas can be ordered for you. Canvas has become quite expensive in recent years. As this book goes to press (1990), canvas adequate to cover your kayak will cost in the neighborhood of $130. Even with added painting costs, this is a reasonable figure compared with alternative covering materials. In any case, if you are careful in laying and cutting out the cloth, your scrap pieces will be enough to make an authentic jumper or pair of nautical trousers for yourself—something not seen in this country for more than a half-century. This, of course, will require a good tailor in your life—also grievously rare!

Regardless of which kayak you are building, you must have two lengths of 4-foot wide, 10-ounce duck canvas. Each length, however, must be 1 ½ feet longer than the boat it is to cover. For example, if your kayak frame is 17 feet long, then you need a 37-foot-long roll of 4-foot-wide, 10-ounce duck canvas. Cut exactly in half, this will yield

Figure 6-1. The framework shrouded in her canvas.

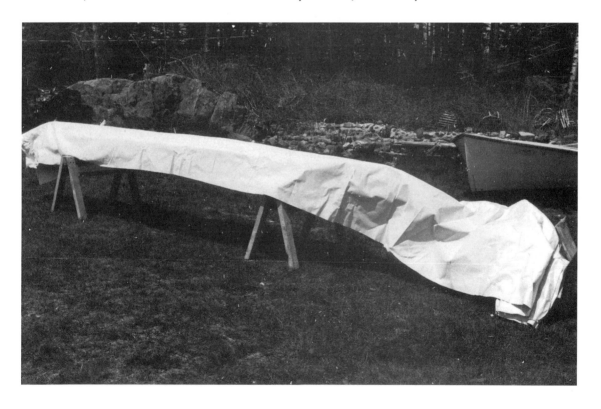

Canvas, Carlins, Stringers, and Paint   69

two lengths each 18 ½ feet long, one length for the bottom and the other for the deck.

Set your kayak frame upside down across the sawhorses such that the frame bears at deck widths that give good lateral stability; one-quarter of the length inward from either end will be about right. This isn't "rocket" science; you will find yourself shifting the relative boat and sawhorse positions often to get various advantages throughout this stage of the project.

Lay a centered length of canvas over the length of the frame backbone, allowing equal overlap (about 9 inches) at either end. First, right at the curve of one stem (over the scarf area) hammer a tack through the canvas, centered into the stem wood. For the 17-footer ⅜-inch copper tacks are best; ½-inch copper tacks for larger boats. (Note: Staples and staple guns may be used, preferably employing Monel or stainless steel staples, which saves time but nothing else. Ordinary staples will rapidly corrode, weep rust stains, and compromise the craft.)

Go to the other stem, grasp the canvas, and pull hard on it, stretching the canvas longitudinally so that the cloth wrinkles moderately down the midline. Holding the fabric firmly in position, drive a copper tack through the cloth into the mid-curve of the stem, just as you did at the other end. The dexterity required for this is not so challenging as it may seem. One hand never leaves the canvas. While that hand stretches the canvas, the other hand positions the tack through the cloth, which holds it in place long enough for you to quickly grasp your hammer and tap the fastener into position. Correctly done, one or two gentle, more or less symmetrical stretch folds should run along the cloth on both sides of the centerline.

This sets up the bottom canvas for lateral, athwartships stretching and tacking to the gunwale strips. This lateral work needs to be done systematically, a few tacks driven at a time from side to side. The watchwords here are *evenness* and *consistency*—keeping all of the stretch-strains in the cloth equally distributed throughout the cloth surface as it is stretched and fastened down the length of the kayak.

The canvas must be tacked to the gunwale strips on both sides, at 1 ½-inch intervals down the length of the boat. Begin amidships and, if you work by yourself, drive no more than a half-dozen tacks on a side or toward one direction of the craft at a time. Move back and forth from one side to the other, alternating progress toward one stem and the other. This procedure will abet the need to maintain canvas tension as the boat shape converges at bow and stern. It's tiring work for, while the pinching and tugging should not be violent, they should be insistent

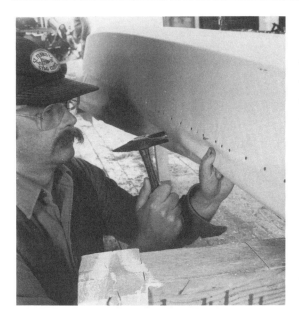

Figure 6-2. Tacking along the sides at intervals, here also showing the "intertacking" used to remove those little pestiferous wrinkles that creep in.

Figure 6-3. A visiting tractor dealer demonstrates canvas overlapping at the stems. PHOTO BY RICK STAFFORD.

and your fingers soon become fatigued and chaffed by the strength and coarseness of the cloth. The point is to move along either side toward the ends while keeping all wrinkles out of the canvas. Some tacks will have to be popped out and redriven, for, as you go back and forth from side to side, new wrinkles have an insidious way of appearing between tacks on the side opposite from where you work. It is an evolutionary thing and takes some patience. But, with doggedness and thoughtful force, it works. Patience! You will drive more than 200 tacks before the bottom is secured. You might as well enjoy them!

As your tacking efforts approach the ends of the boat you will find that a lot of superfluous canvas accumulates in large, increasingly inconvenient folds. This is supposed to happen; it is a natural function of the converging sides. Interrupt the tacking procedure about two feet from the stemheads, just abaft and below the location of the stem-curve tacks. Then stand out from the end(s) of the setup and pull and center the excess canvas toward you. Slit the excess canvas with a very sharp knife near to the tack at the stem scarf. Do not approach this tack closer than about ¾ inch. Then pull the extra canvas from one side across the stem timber and, using your eye and some tugging this way and that, determine where the cloth should lie on the stem timber to orient the material for a smooth adjoining skin to the end of the craft.

Figure 6-4. Trimming off the excess hull canvas.

Tack the canvas into place, running the tacks in a line down the outside edge of the stem timber from whence the canvas comes, and then trim off the excess cloth. It is good practice to tack the canvas to the gunwales on the working side before following the same procedure on the opposite side. Handle the excess cloth there in the same way. Be very careful not to allow your knife to damage the fabric beneath when trimming off the excess canvas from the second side.

Perform the same operations at the other end of the boat. Then trim the excess hull canvas. Study Figures 6–3, 6–4, and 6–5; they should help you get through this canvasing procedure.

THE COCKPIT CARLINS

Cockpit carlins are next. And once again you have some choices to make! What shape and size of cockpit do you want? The carlins, the timbers that underlie the cockpit, determine the kind of structural environment in which you will sit—how you experience the boat and what you do with it. The cockpit is headquarters and most important to the success of the craft. Though based on a native Greenland kayak, the rather large cathedral-arch–shaped cockpit of this boat as designed makes this version a family recreational craft for use near shore in relatively calm waters. If your desire is to take the kayak offshore, into challenging seas, then you will want a smaller, tighter cockpit with a round, oval, or ellipsoidal shape capable of securely fitting a paddler's skirt, which the designed shaped does not easily do.

The length of the cockpit space is limited by the distance between the deck beams immediately forward and aft. If you want a shorter or longer cockpit, you may adjust the location of the forward deck beam by backing out the screws, breaking the glue seal, and resetting the member where you want it. Since it is located for reasons of weight distribution (center of gravity), the designed location of the after deck beam should remain as shown. As you will see, the width of the cockpit is a matter of your choice and building—anything between what you can squeeze into and nearly the full width of the boat. In any case, boats built for general family use should be built to the design provided. Boats planned for lots of multi-children use or for two adults who like one another a lot call for a longer cockpit. Boats wanted by large persons or by average persons who want or need to take lots of equipment or gear with them will need a cockpit both longer and wider than designed. The cockpit under construction in the photographs of the 18 ½-foot version is very long and wide compared with the designed

Figure 6-5. A trimmed, canvased hull. You'll notice that here the cockpit carlins have been installed. Sometimes I do this before canvasing the hull, sometimes after; experience with both leaves me with a preference for neither. In the text I installed the cockpit carlins after canvasing the hull.

specifications, in order that it may accommodate a rowing machine.

When you have determined how wide you want your cockpit, mark the location of the inside carlin's edge on the forward face of the after cockpit deck beam. Be sure that your marks fall equidistantly from the centerline out and from the gunwale strips in. An off-center cockpit would plague you and the boat for the boat's lifetime!

The fabrication and fitting of the carlins takes a certain amount of fuss and muscling; an assistant can be very helpful. It is perfectly possible to execute the procedure alone, but to do so will be more verbally rich in regard to expletives and epithets. Recruit a friend if possible. In any case, fabricate two carlin butt blocks out of square-sectioned stock of the same dimension as the carlin stock, which should be in square section the same as the strip stock is wide, and install them at an angle that conforms with the camber of the after deck at the cockpit after deck beam, one carlin stock width short of the marked line. (Read that last sentence again and think of all the dead technical writers.) Then install the butt blocks with glue, end-screws through the gunwale strips, and at least one screw through each butt block into the deck beam. As you will see, these butt blocks provide an anchor and locator for the after ends of the carlin timbers as you bend, cut, and mount them into position.

Cut off the carlin stock about six inches longer than the length of the cockpit space. Then, with a ripsaw, rip the carlin stock about half its length from the forward end. Ripsaw with the grain, parallel with the annual rings of the wood. This will allow the wood to bend easily, fairly, and symmetrically into position. An assistant now comes in very handy to hold the after-end of the carlin stock in place against the after deck beam and butt block, while you muscle the carlin into whatever curve you want the forward end of the cockpit to have. When you have achieved the curve you want, hold the curve securely with one hand, and with the other mark the double-bevel cut-off location on the bifurcated wood with a pencil. Relieve the bend and take the now-marked carlin stock to a vise.

Gently but firmly clamp the sawn, marked carlin stock in the vise such that you can rebend the piece more or less into the shape it is to take in the boat, and so that the double-bevel pencil marks on either side of the saw cut again coincide. Holding the piece thus in position, cut to and along the pencil lines, preferably with a fine backsaw or dovetailing saw. Relieve the piece from the vise and return it to the boat. There, spring the carlin piece into position, double-check it, and then predrill for at least one screw fastener through the forward end of the split stock, and another through the back of the after cockpit deck

Figure 6-6. The carlins slotted with the grain to aid in the bending. The various screws that go into and across the slotting later renew most of the strength lost in doing it.

beam into the end grain of the piece. Relieve the piece, glue both ends, remount into position, and fasten.

Follow this same procedure in fabricating and installing the other carlin, taking special precautions to see that its curve and angle to the boat is the same as that of its companion member.

The spaces that have been created on both sides of the frame between the cockpit carlins and gunwale strips, when covered with canvas, will become the waterways, or side decks of the boat. These spaces need to be reinforced with two or three (depending on the length of your cockpit) waterway deck beams fitted between the gunwale strips and carlins. They want a somewhat rhomboidal profile and are installed, after trial-and-error whittling and fussing, with glue and screws in the usual manner. You may need somewhat longer screws to penetrate the carlins and still get good holding into the end grain of these short deck beams. I usually just give the drilling a bit more countersink. Study Figures 5–7a and 5–7b for short deck beam details.

A Note on the Sole of the Boat

Now that you have established a place to sit in your kayak, you need to consider the structure on which to sit. Clearly, the floor timber, keelson, stringers, and canvas bottom matrix makes for neither a comfortable nor a particularly smart place to sit. Your buttocks would concentrate most of your weight on a very small portion of the lower structure where, working in opposition to the buoyancy of the rest of the craft, few fastenings and small glue surfaces would have to bear nearly all of the paddler's weight and movements. You need to build a *sole,* an interior deck, that bears your weight when sitting and perhaps also bears the placement of legs and feet. Again you have options, depending on your needs and priorities.

If you want a large sole permanently fixed into the craft, then you should build it in now, before added deck frameworking is installed and makes the work more difficult. If you want either a small sole that accommodates just the sitting area of the cockpit, or an unattached and narrow sole that can be removed from the boat, then you can delay its fabrication until after the kayak shell is finished. There are advantages and disadvantages to each option. Large built-in soles allow greater flexibility in paddler positioning, multiple paddlers, protection of gear and equipment from ambient water that gets into the boat, and prevent harm coming to the boat from feet and legs, including from sandy sneakers that can wreck havoc when scraped on the inside surface of raw canvas. The major disadvantages of large, fixed soles are added overall weight and difficult access to the bilges of the boat for cleaning, drying, and retrieval of lost objects.

If you choose to install a large sole, do it before finishing the deck framework. Use inch-wide resilient stock such as pine or spruce, planed to quarter-inch thickness, spaced at half-inch intervals, and screwed directly to the top of the floor timbers. Some play in the laths does no harm, so fastening at every other floor timber is adequate. If you desire either a small cockpit sole, or a long narrow one that can be removed from the boat, longitudinal members are the same. A removable sole requires cross-members, sole beams, of its own, spaced at intervals that will place them between floor timbers when installed into the boat.

THE DECK STRINGERS

Six deck members must be established to support and give shape to the canvas deck, three forward of the cockpit and three aft. Use the standard strip stock you used for the hull framework. Keep in mind that you want the deck to be fair, even, and beautiful, without odd lumps and bumps. Begin with the two kingstrips, the stringers that run down the deck centerline from bow forepeak to the head of the carlins, and from the center of the after cockpit deck beam to the afterpeak of the stern stem timber. Depending on how elevated you have made the fore end of the carlins, and how much camber you have given the cockpit deck beam, you may or may not wish to notch and house the cockpit ends of the kingstrips and deck stringers. I did do so on the boat in Figures 5–6a and 5–6b, but notice that it creates a flattened effect on the deck profile forward and aft of the cockpit area. I deemed this proper for a craft that would be rowed often. Strictly paddled craft of traditional form need not have the deck longitudinal members notched and let into the cockpit structure. Similarly, the outer ends of the kingstrips need not be let into the heads of the stem timbers. Cut the kingstrips to length, fit them, predrill, glue, and fasten them into position.

They do need to be faired and sanded to a kind shape at the ends. Give the stem-head ends a light planing and sanding to a blunted and fair point. Remove and sand the upper corners of the inboard ends so that they will not stress the deck canvas, and fair the actual ends into the inside of the carlin apex, and the inside surface of the cockpit after deck beam.

Then install the four deck stringers, about which there are two special features. First, notice in Figure 6–7 that the deck stringers are not faired into the forepeak; neither are the after deck stringers faired into the stern. They terminate as floating ends well aft of the stemhead, and are rather severely planed, rasped, and sanded to a fair shape to prevent too much proudness through the canvas that will cover them. Second, all four deck stringers need to be edge-set in fair curves between

Figure 6-7. Detail of tapering used on the deck stringers to avoid hard edges.

stems and cockpit. These members are located by striking half-distance marks on the deck beams between the inside edge of the gunwale strips and kingstrips on both sides of the boat, both forward and aft of the cockpit. By adding half of the width of the strip stock to either the inside or outside of these marks (be consistent!), you derive visible marks for proper placement of the deck stringers.

Though the edge-set of the deck stringers is not especially severe, it is still a good idea to mock-up each strip into position with clamps, and to predrill the screw holes. Install the members by fastening through glue placed on the deck beams only. This will lend evolution to the process, rather than panic because not everything can be done at once and because a mess is created by dangling strip ends smearing glue over the work. Work progressively from one end of each stringer strip to the other. Finally remove the inboard corners of these strips, and sand and fair them to the cockpit carlin and deck beam inboard surfaces, just as you did for the kingstrips.

Clean out the boat! All kinds of chips and sawdust will have worked their way into the bilges by now. These are pollutants that later on can collect moisture, sponsor mildew, and create bumps and chafing surfaces that endanger the canvas skin. Pieces of metal and loose fasteners are especially insidious. Vacuum the inside of the boat. Turn the craft upside down and whack along the craft with your hand to loosen material that has crept under the keelson and stringers. Then vacuum the inside of the boat again. Make the boat as tidy as possible, for once you have installed the deck canvas only the cockpit area will be directly accessible for a long time—probably, hopefully, for years.

THE DECK CANVAS

Canvasing the deck is much easier and more straightforward than canvasing the bottom. Again, the canvas should be firmly stretched and pinned at the ends, directly onto the stemheads, on and along the centerline. The canvas should cover the entire boat, including the cockpit. As you did in applying the bottom covering, progressively and evenly tack the deck canvas to the gunwale strips, this time through the bottom canvas as well. Begin amidships and move back and forth from side to side outward toward the ends, all the time gently but firmly pulling on the canvas to maintain even tension and to prevent folds or loose spots. Be sure to feel your way along the gunwales, so you can place the deck canvas tacks more or less evenly between the bottom canvas tacks.

When the deck canvas has been tacked into position, fix a pencil into

your carpenter's dividers, set the gap at ¾ inch with the pencil slightly recessed. Then, using the pointed tip as a guide along the top of the outside edge of the gunwale, strike a trimming line on to the excess deck canvas around the entire perimeter of the boat. Be as careful and consistent as possible for the overlapped canvas that is left must be painted and later covered by a rubbing strake. Retrimming later on will be inconvenient—indeed a hassle.

A similar but wider trimming line needs to be drawn onto the portion of canvas that covers the cockpit area. Your dividers can be used for this, but it is just as easy to use your best working hand, holding a pencil as you normally do, extending your pinky (little finger) out as a guide to follow the carlin edge as you strike a line about four inches inside of the cockpit perimeter, all the way around it. This will allow enough excess canvas after trimming to hold and tension the material as you tack it to the inside of the carlins.

Figures 6-8A-D. Deck canvas is installed and trimmed, a space line is established out from the carlin (felt through the canvas), slit with a sharp knife, and stapled or tacked into the carlin all around the cockpit.

The trim lines that you have struck must now be cut. Use your very best knife, razor sharp. With benign confidence and care, grasp the excess material and progressively, at a right angle, run your knife down and through the canvas exactly along the pencil lines, being sure that the blade tip does not nick any underlying hull covering. A sharp knife runs cleanly through the canvas as if it were a zipper; it's an oddly sensual, satisfying process, even if a bit nerve-racking, around the outside of the boat.

The outside canvas overlap should fair to the hull pretty well. Do not worry about tension folds that appear around some of the tacks. This is normal, and they will shrink once painted and be covered by the rubbing strake. It is the canvas that overlaps around the cockpit carlins and deck beam that now requires your attention.

If you have opted for the cathedral-arch cockpit shape, as designed and shown, you have three corners that require corner-slitting of the cloth; the fore-end peak and the two quarters at either side of the after-end cockpit deck beam. Round, ovoid, or ellipsoidal cockpit shapes do not have corners, and so require slitting of the canvas at regular intervals all around their perimeter. The point is to get the canvas to lay as perfectly as possible all around the cockpit without allowing the necessary slits to reach or appear at deck level, where they can create problems (tearing and leaking) later on. Slit the canvas only to within $3/8$ inch of the corners (if you chose the arch-shaped cockpit) or perimeter edges (of rounded shape variations). After it is painted, the natural elasticity and tolerance of the cloth will permit completely tight installation of the coamings that later will go over these compromises of the material. Keep the slit ends below the deckline.

Using the same tack-spacing intervals as you used along the gunwales, tack the canvas to the inside of the carlins and along the lower edge of the cockpit after deck beam. Then use the lower edge of the whole system as a guide for your very sharp knife to cut off all excess canvas, all around the cockpit.

In addition to being beautiful to look at and exciting to contemplate, the boat is ready to fill, prime, and paint!

PAINTING THE BOAT

Canvas is an organic material that presents a rather rough surface that needs to be protected from chafe, waterproofed, and decorated. The techniques that I prescribe here are the old-fashioned ones, using traditional oil-based coatings. These have been used on canvas for more than two centuries, and work well if the surface is not excessively

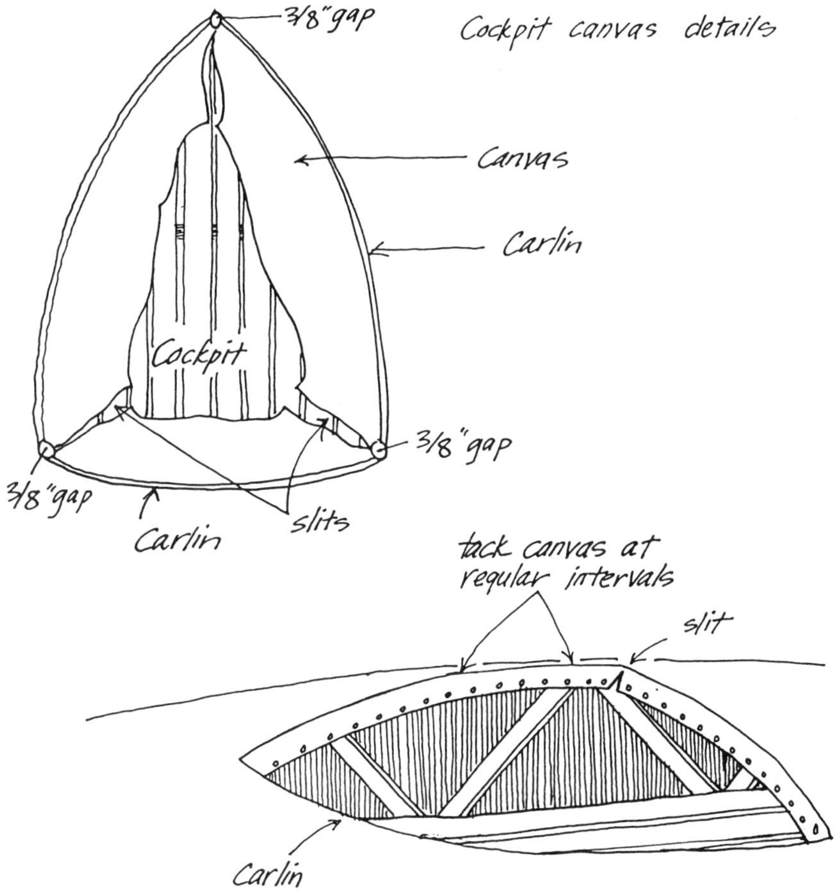

Figure 6-9. Corner slitting
the deck canvas.

Cockpit canvas details

3/8"gap

Canvas

Carlin

Cockpit

3/8"gap

3/8"gap

Carlin

slits

tack canvas at
regular intervals

slit

Carlin

abused or unnecessarily exposed to the elements, especially sunlight.
Alternative, possibly superior coatings are available. Just as contemporary skins such as Kevlar or aircraft heat-shrinkable Dacron may
be considered for the hull covering, various elastic and UV-filtered
polymolecular coatings, such as polyurethane, can be used. I commend
them to you, with good wishes. In the spirit of this craft as designed
and this book as tendered, we continue forward into the past, creating a good boat that requires as much care in upkeep as it does in
fabrication and use.

First, you must "kill the weave." This old expression refers to the
roughness of canvas duck and the necessity to fill the tiny interstices in
the cloth before you achieve a surface that can be worked with
sandpaper without compromising the strength of the material. Years
ago I did this using old porch paint—still not a bad idea, if you include
some added filler, such as chalk powder, and extra dryer. The major
yacht paint manufacturers make commercial fillers from time to time,

but on a proprietary basis—and expensive—to local chandleries, boat-yards, and marinas. If you can find Boatyard Sanding Sealer #144, by Interlux, for example, you are gold-plated. It is great stuff, for only two coats of it completely fills 10-ounce, canvas weave, leaving a surface that sands perfectly and hosts oil-based marine paints with enthusiasm. Since #144 is no more, you need to find a substitute with its characteristics available locally. Begin with a high-grade, flat-white paint and moderately add extra filler and dryer to it, all the while stirring the mixture until it attains a consistency of smooth pancake batter. Paint it into the canvas with aggressive, poking strokes; then brush out the dobs as you go. You will need a minimum of two coats. Fill the canvas, and then allow the last fill-coat to dry thoroughly.

This renders a sound, sandable surface. Number 80-grit garnet sandpaper is just right for the job. It is coarse enough to smooth the surface quickly, is easily controlled so as not to abrade the cloth without your noticing, and leaves a surface that holds finish color well. Sand your canvas kayak completely, with affection.

Since a decade or more should pass before a canvas boat requires a new skin, only enough paint to kill the weave and color the boat should be used. All paints applied to organic cloth develop cracks. Think of it: Imagine oil paintings, almost always on gessoed canvas, left outside—indeed regularly soaked in water (salt water!)—and then stored under a tree all summer. They would crack, and quickly. The inevitability of this fate for your kayak's canvas skin can be reduced right from the start by using only thin coats of very good paint. Anticipate that a new coat of paint will be needed every year, especially if the boat is stored outdoors between uses and ambient humidity is allowed to have its way with the canvas. True, the craft would look a bit better if the paint were built-up right at first, but the overall, long-term health of the boat is improved if the initial color is left at two coats well-applied. Later coats in later years are given the job of providing the deepened beauty this boat takes on through time.

I sand the kayaks each spring, apply one coat of color as thinly as possible, and then add one coat of thinned, UV-filtered, spar varnish for gloss and protection for the paint. (For more on varnish selection, see Chapter 7.) After several years these layers add up in thickness, weight, and pestiferousness. Conservatism at the beginning helps. Let a bit of the canvas texture show through the paint the first year or two.

When you have built up the color and surface you like, you are ready for the dresswork—the orchestra of finish woodworking and touches that transform a good, sound craft into a beautiful, desirable boat to be admired and envied.

7

Finish Woodwork, Varnishing, and Paddles and Oars

For practical purposes, you now have a kayak. You can use it. But it is not finished in the proper sense, and it is best if you do not give in to the temptation to "give it just a little try." Keep it in the shop, and work on.

FINISH WOODWORK

To be complete your kayak needs a keel, rubbing strakes (also called *rails* or *guards*), and a coaming. Not only do these pieces dress up the craft, they add significant strength, protection, and utility. Because the aesthetic effect is so powerful and lovely, I suggest that you varnish the finish woodwork and therefore choose clear and straight-grained hardwoods or tropical woods for their construction. White or red oak, white ash (stained or unstained), either Caribbean (Honduran) or Southeast Asian (Philippine) mahoganies are all appropriate woods to use, are available, and will work well. If weight-saving is a critical consideration, clear spruce will work fine for the keel and rails but will not be so resistant to the hazards of use—especially beaching. Use hardwoods for the coaming, if at all possible, and, in the spirit of treading lightly on this earth, select domestic varities. We take them one at a time.

The Keel

The keel has several functions. It increases the longitudinal strength of the backbone by orders of magnitude. It provides protection against abrasion or holing of the skin by presenting a striking and scraping surface to the environment. Its addition to the hull along the bottom centerline provides "lateral resistance" to the water, which allows the kayak to track—go in a straight line rather than slough about—as paddling forces are applied from side to side. Finally, it gives the lower profile of the boat a hard visual edge and, with or without scarfed-in stem dress pieces, looks terrific.

The easiest keel to get out and install is of spruce (Sitka, white, or red), quarter-sawn the full length of the boat including stems, with the annual-ring grain horizontal to the waterline. If not in too great a section, this wood thus sawn will allow dry cold-bending around the curvature of the stems. A perfect and lucky piece of white pine may do the same, but could be a heartbreaker as well as a keel-breaker. All other wood species require wet hot-bending.

In all cases the stock should be the same width as the strip stock that was used for the keelson. The depth, or thickness, is a matter of choice, but anything greater than ½ inch will preclude dry cold-bending and will begin to add weight to the craft without an advantageous return. Any keel actually can go a bit thinner, say ¹⁄₁₆ inch less than the depth of the interior frame strip stock, without harming the craft's integrity.

Figure 7-1. Cross-section of the finished keel's chamfered edge.

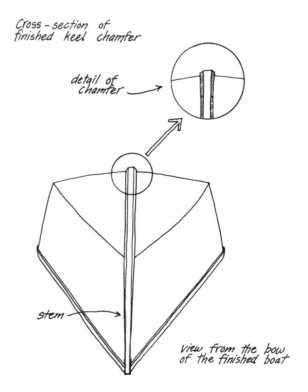

Cross-section of finished keel chamfer

detail of chamfer →

stem →

view from the bow of the finished boat

Wood and Canvas Kayak Building

Too, it is best to shape the keel stock the way you want it before you apply it to the boat. I suggest that you chamfer the edges to about $\frac{3}{16}$-inch depth off the corners, $\frac{1}{4}$ inch down the depth and across the width. This is not an easy job on such a long thin stock. I hold the timber to the workbench and progressively chamfer the stock on either side with a sharp block plane set to a fairly large cut, releasing and reholding the wood as I progress down the length. Minor unevenness I fair with sandpaper later. Other kinds of planes and routers, a spokeshave, and even a draw knife with a depth-stop attached can accomplish the same task. The rails must receive the same treatment.

Dry cold-bending is simply a matter of centering the stock so that you are sure there is a little extra length at either end, and fastening the keel from amidships toward the ends with oversized screws (gauged not to penetrate the inside surface of the keelson) at six-inch intervals along the straight run of the bottom. Then, with the help of an assistant, very carefully bend the keel strip slowly but surely around the bend of the stem, countersinking screw holes and driving fastenings at relatively close intervals—between three and four inches apart—until finally a last fastening can be driven into the apex of the stemhead. Repeat this procedure at the opposite end. Oversized screws are wanted here because of the added thickness of two layers of painted cloth and, at the stems, two courses of copper tack heads. I usually use $\frac{3}{4}$-inch, #8 bronze screws for this work. It looks like overkill, but when you consider that these outside dress pieces are not aided by glue (the keel would not hold to a painted canvas), the temptation is to go even heavier in the fastening department. At these specifications, I have never had finishwork let go or a boat leak because of the system.

Other woods and thickness dimension require wet hot-bending methods. A wooden-boat builder's steam box system will work, but it requires installing your keel in two sections scarfed together. Steaming both ends of, say, a 19-foot-long strip of wood is impractical, even if you could get out the piece and bend both ends in the couple of minutes that it takes to bend and fasten an end. In any case, scarfing a keel timber in effect betrays one of its most important functions—strength. A much more practical means of wet hot-bending is to install the keel strip from amidships as before, allowing enough play toward the ends to permit several layers of cotton cloth to be wrapped around the strip area to be bent, and then to thoroughly soak the cloth with boiling hot water for about 10 minutes. I have used this system on red oak, white ash, and Philippine mahogany with great success. Two large tea kettles of water were enough in every case. Again with an assistant, work with dispatch as soon as the soaking cloth is removed to bend the member

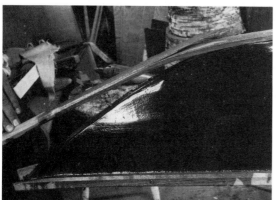

Figures 7-2A-D. Sawing out a keel from an expensive mahogany plank, soaking the strip in hot water, breaking the first effort, and succeeding in the second with ash. The mahogany made excellent rails however. Don't use a power driver, as I did here; hand power only as I explain in the text. Learn from my mistakes.

around the curvature all the way, holding the end down firmly in place as countersunk fastenings are driven. If the wood resists the bend, soak it some more until it cooperates. The water must be near boiling hot, and enough time must be allowed for the heat to penetrate the timber and the moisture to soak at least the outer wood cell layers.

Use only a hand screwdriver! And bear in mind, as you bear down on the screws you must drive, that just a fraction of an inch away is a soft, highly vulnerable canvas skin that will be punctured in an instant if your tool slips out of the screw slots. Be direct, firm, and concentrate on what you are doing!

Separate stem dress pieces, scarfed into the keel just below the stem curves, allow you to customize the end profiles of your craft. They entail extra work, but the most attractive canvas kayaks I have seen inevitably sport custom stem dress pieces, both bow and stern. An example of this is shown in the 17-footer undergoing repairs in Chapter 8 (Figure 8–6). Having this choice gives you another opportunity to make this kayak uniquely yours and a lot of design freedom without affecting the integrity of the boat. It allows you to use exotic figured woods, to make a curved stem into a straight or clippered one. Carvings and figureheads are possible. After a glance at the paddler, people look at the profile of a kayak, particularly the ends and especially the bow. It is the signature of the boat, and here you can sign it.

If you choose to customize your stems, it is a good idea to get out your stem dress pieces before you install the regular keel piece. The keel end-scarfs can go anywhere within about five inches of the stem curve, and leaving the keel until last provides some degrees of freedom in fabricating the dress woodwork. Let science serve art.

There are three mandatory requirements for the end dress pieces: (1) They have to fit the curvature of the stems exactly; (2) They have to be of a dimension that allows adequate fastening to the stem timbers; (3) They have to taper at the lower end to the thickness of the keel and receive a scarf that marries the piece to the keel.

If you are going to all the trouble to create custom stem pieces, then you may as well think in terms of a bright, varnished finish for them and so give the grain of the wood you use careful consideration. Most people have no choice but to use straight-grained wood, in which case try to choose a piece of quarter-sawn wood that shows off the grain to best advantage. Natural sweeps in wood from curved tree branches look beautiful when varnished. Apple and oak trees are good sources,

Figure 7-3. An outer stempiece scarfed to the keel in an old 17-footer, a veteran of eight years, 14-odd coats of paint and varnish, lots of abuse and repairs—and considerable affection.

as are cherry trees (indeed, almost any fruitwood), and any of the larches cut low in the tree bole. If you do not have a band saw, seek one out and buy either service or time on it. Rough-sawn stock should be wide enough to finish-plane to the frame stock width. Plane the stock or have it planed to frame stock width.

The first line and cut on the stock should be to the curve of the stem—above and beyond the stemhead, below and beyond the keel line. This can be mocked out with a piece of corrugated cardboard, a pencil, and a scissors or knife by trial and error until it fits the stem area perfectly. Using the established cardboard edge as a template, trace the line onto the stock, leaving enough space on the stock to execute your design intentions. Be as flamboyant or modest as you wish, but keep in mind principles of proportion and practicality. Kayaks are trim, light, fast boats, and do not benefit from especially heavy and ornate stem dress pieces. The dresswork used on the repair example in Chapter 8 (Figure 8–6) is of straight-grained red oak with a simple, obtuse chamfer along the outer edge. It looks great. One very good book about wood carving is *The Shipcarver's Handbook,* by Jay Hanna (WoodenBoat, Brooklin, ME, 1988; available from International Marine Publishing Co.).

When you are satisfied with your stem piece, be sure that it fits exactly the stem curvature. Then cut off and dress the head of the piece in an attractive manner, and sand the piece smooth. At the lower terminus of the bow dress piece, saw an overlapping scarf surface at as severe an angle as you can manage—five-to-one (5:1) length to depth is desirable. Do the same for the stern stem dress piece, except underlap the scarf surface.

Since the ends of the boat are covered in canvas, use of through-bolts to fasten the stem dress pieces is not a possibility; the canvas prevents inside access to the bolts so you cannot tighten them. You have to use screws, not a bad thing given the depth of the underlying stem timbers. The screws are apt to be long, and especially purchased to fit the dimensions of your dress pieces. Whatever, countersink them deeply, driving the fasteners so that they reach nearly to the inside surface of the stem timbers. Five or six longer screws and four or five shorter ones will be needed to fix the member soundly into position.

Then, fit the keel to the stem dress pieces. Begin at the forward end, cutting and fitting the keel stock to the overlapping scarf at the bow. Once that fit is established, carefully sight, mark, and cut a scarf at the stern end to overlap the dress piece's underlap. Fit, predrill, glue at the scarfs, and fasten the keel timber into place. Round over, or increase the chamfer on, the edges of the keel. Then sand the keel fair into the stem dress pieces, taking special pains to fair the scarfs. Be careful that your sanding and fussing does not scrape the painted canvas.

Use glued wood plugs to fill the deeply countersunk screw holes in the stem dress pieces. You can purchase plugs to the dimension of your countersunk holes at good hardware stores, woodworking supply outlets, and wooden boat shops. Or you can purchase the appropriate plug die (that chucks into any drillpress) and make your own. Ordinary plastic wood fills and dresses the regular fastening holes along the keel length, *and serves all of the other filling needs of the finish woodwork.* Apply the stuff generously, let it dry thoroughly (overnight), and then sand through a couple of paper grits to a smooth finish that renders all of the screw holes round and fair to the wood.

The Rails

The functions of the rails are to add lateral strength to the boat, to cover and protect the cloth overlaps of the hull and deck canvas covers along the underlying gunwale strip, to provide fender protection to the craft from alongside hazards, and to give aesthetic definition to the sheerline of the boat.

Unless you anticipate especially hard and regular use of your kayak against wharfs, docks, rocks, or other boats, do not give your rails full (framework) strip depths. Three-eighths (⅜) inch for larger craft and 5/16 inch for 17-footers is very adequate for boats intended for normal use. In any case, these depths allow you to use the fastenings you regularly employed in building the framework. Again, as for the keel timber, it is best to give rails whatever section you want before installing them. Half-rounding them is OK, but a chamfered section, using the same methods as for the keel, is better. Chamfers catch the light beautifully and visually set off the boat in a compelling way. Make sure that your rail timbers are centered to the boat, with overlapping length at either end.

Attach the rails beginning amidships, working out toward the ends of the boat. The help of an assistant comes in handy as you predrill and drive the first few screws. After that, move forward and aft along the boat, drilling and fastening a few screws at a time at six-inch intervals. You will find that some edge-setting of the wood is needed as you approach the ends, but it is not severe and the wood will accommodate you. Stresses such as these that you build into the boat give the craft unity and liveliness. Kayaks are like people; not only are they of organic materials, they too develop character by distributing the stresses they cannot resolve.

Both bent-on keels and rails should be terminated at the stemheads with simple rounding over, using a fine rasp and sandpaper. Since the outermost fastenings are fixed within ¾ inch of the ends, significant thinning of these finish woodwork members at the ends is neither practical nor desirable. Rails can be let in to custom stem pieces, but this technique usually results in a ponderous, shelf-like structure at the ends, out of proportion to the rest of the craft.

The Coaming

The coaming is in effect a fence that surrounds the cockpit. Made of relatively wide, thin strips of wood, the recommended cathedral-arch design, shown in the photographs, is fastened to the sides of the carlins and after cockpit deck beam and reinforced at the quarters with triangular-sectioned, corner fill pieces and at the head with an apex piece. Fabrication and installation of the coaming constitutes the most sophisticated woodworking demanded in this project and, while not difficult, it does require your concentration and patience if the results are to be strong and beautiful. Work carefully and systematically. Double-check all fits, and remember that it is always possible to remove existing wood from a piece of stock and impossible to replace it once it lands as scrap and chips on the shop floor. Expect many trips back and forth between boat and bench.

Figure 7-4. Scribing a coaming.

Wood and Canvas Kayak Building

The coaming functions in several important ways. The strength that it gives the cockpit is critical. Think about it; here is a boat that is going to end up weighing about 70 pounds, less than half the weight of the average adult paddler who will get in and out of the boat, hopefully thousands of times, each time placing nearly his or her entire weight on the coamings when embarking or emerging from the craft. Unadorned carlins could not possibly take such treatment. Coamings also join the rails in giving added lateral strength to the boat. The raised, vertical surface of the coaming helps keep the cockpit dry, both from wave splash and from the drips that usually attend paddling. This same surface also gives good body-bearing to paddlers, who, as they become proficient, more and more think of the boat as part of their body, and often use the coaming as a torquing and impetus surface in their maneuvering. The coamings often become arm and paddle rests, and thus protect the deck from ambient scraping and chafe. Finally the varnished woodwork of the structure creates an enormously satisfying visual environment for paddler and onlooker alike.

Coaming Side Pieces   The stock used for the coaming should be both decorative and quite deep. Up close, it is the cockpit coaming that people look at, so it should look good. Extra depth of the stock is necessary because of the forward and aft vertical sweep of the carlins. Your stock needs to be at least five inches wide, or come from a naturally curved source—again, large fruitwood or oak tree branches, well seasoned. The stock needs to be of a thin hardwood because (1) the side pieces have to be bent into position, (2) the after piece able to take the stresses from the paddler's back, and (3) the whole able to fill all member functions. Any coaming stock more than ¼ inch thick would be almost impossible to fit, and would look ill-proportioned. I have used white ash, red oak, apple, longleaf yellow pine, and Philippine mahogany with equal success. Stock at least five inches deep, long enough to provide the side and after pieces, and finish-planed to ⁵/₃₂ inch, is the order.

Square off one end of the stock. Take the plank to the boat, set the squared end against an after corner of the cockpit where a carlin joins the deck beam, and, standing beside the boat facing forward, let your thumb bear on the stock and your fingers reach under and behind the carlin. Squeeze the coaming stock up against the carlin and, with your other hand, place and hold the stock plank in a position where it fairs at the apex of the cockpit aperture. Then either have a friend mark a line vertical from that point or fix your eye intently at that point, quickly release the tension, and mark the line yourself. This line does not have to be exactly vertical; approximate and straight are all that is required.

Cut the stock at this line. Return the cut coaming blank piece to the boat, and muscle it into position. If you cut the forward apex line properly, the blank should just about spring fair and hold itself against the ends where it is to go, less a bit of spring that now needs to be clamped against the carlins with small clamps. With a little tapping and adjustment of the clamps, place the coaming blank such that its entire lower edge falls below the lower line of the carlin and the upper edge stands well above the line of the deck, all along its length.

You now must decide how high you want your coaming—how much it is to rise above the deck canvas. Two and a half inches is about average. Lower coamings let in quite a lot of wave splash and reduce psychological security; higher ones get in the way of paddling and are subject to breakage. One and three-fourths inches (1 ¾) to 2 ¾ inches are your practical limits.

Whatever you decide, set your carpenter's dividers at the measurement you've chosen and, running the point along the deck, scribe an evenly curved line on the coaming blank. Then, with a short stubby pencil up under the clamped piece and using the bottom edge of the carlin as a guide, scribe an evenly curved line along the backside of the blank. These two scribed lines will determine the top and bottom edges of the coaming. Undo the clamps, unspring the coaming blank, and return it to the workbench.

With either band saw or bowsaw, saw to the lines on the coaming blank, finishing the convex edge with a finish plane or spokeshave and the concave edge with a convex spokeshave. Return the piece to the boat, and make sure that it is going to be satisfactory—that it fits and looks the way you want it to when its bottom edge is faired to the lower carlin edge. Thus checked, use your new coaming section as a template to trace on the plank stock for the other coaming side piece; cut it out and finish it as a duplicate of the piece you have worked so hard to create. Make them as exactly alike as possible. Finish both with a light sanding.

One at a time, spring and clamp each side coaming piece into position, predrill and countersink screw holes at three-inch intervals, and drive the fastenings home. As with the keel, we are not using epoxy or adhesive because it won't adhere to the painted canvas; screws are the only fastening game in this part of the kayak. You will notice that there is a V-shaped gap between the side coaming pieces at the apex, the

Figure 7-5. Getting out the coaming.

Figure 7-6. The coamings ready to install.

forward end of the cockpit (Figure 7–7). This is normal, and will be filled and faired with a carved apex piece, momentarily and in due course.

The Coaming Back Piece   You must now get out and install the back piece of the coaming. Whether or not you have given the cockpit beam a compound curvature, this little piece of wood can give trouble in the way that it fits against the after ends of the coaming side pieces, which have a way of slightly flaring outward from the centerline. So, your challenge is to fit a back piece blank from stock down between the side pieces as they naturally set and against the deck beam, whether it's curved or not. If the deck beam is not curved forward and aft, you can simply take measurements and angles from the cockpit and transfer them to the stock, the depth of which will allow the necessary freedom to strike upper and lower transverse lines. If the deck beam is

Figure 7-7. Maple coamings (not recommended), ash backpiece (highly recommended) dressed with apple corners (nice).

compound-curved, developing a piece of template cardboard will save time, stock, and frustration.

When you have established the side fit of the blank, clamp it into position and strike the bottom line first, using the same methods you employed on the side pieces. Then clearly mark with a pencil where the back piece meets the top of the after ends of the side pieces. Unclamp the blank and return it to the workbench. There, either by eye or by use of a pencil and string, strike a fair curve to connect the coaming side tick marks. I usually do this by eye, with the intention of striking what would be the cord of a circle about three feet in diameter. Later I moderate this into a slightly more ellipsoidal edge with plane and sandpaper, right on the boat. Saw to the bottom edge line and the upper curved line, and finish with planes, spokeshave, and sandpaper just as you did the side pieces.

Mount, clamp, predrill, and fasten the coaming back piece to the deck beam with screws driven at three-inch intervals, about ¾ inch up from the bottom edge of the back piece face. Then get out and mock up two triangular-sectioned corner pieces to fill the quarters of the coaming unit. Fair the bottoms of these to the carlin side pieces/back piece corners, but leave the tops a bit proud above the corner joints. Use glue and at least two screws to fasten these into position. When the glue has set and cured, use a fine rasp and sandpaper to trim and fair the entire corner into one attractive joint.

At this point you may give the top edge of the back piece whatever finish camber or shape you want. Do not make the top of the back piece too high or severely shaped, for a paddler's back will surely break off any superfluous wood left at the crown of this member. Meanwhile, you have some creative carving to do in getting-out the apex piece of the coaming.

The Apex Piece of the Coaming Now, here is a piece of work! It is not nearly so difficult and complicated as it may appear. The apex piece must fair together the forward ends of the coaming side pieces, and then fair the whole coaming structure to the foredeck in an attractive way. You accomplish this not by trying to create the unit all of a sculptured piece, but by thinking of the assignment as simply a dual-rabbeted wedge that must be fitted vertically to the forward end of the cockpit coaming. Look at the Figure 7–8 series now and study each step as you go through the process; I think it will help.

Looking down into the place where the piece is to go, you will see the wedge that is required, with rabbets on either side to receive the ends of the side coaming pieces (Figure 7–8a). Except for a shallow shelf let in where the wedge should slightly overlap the foredeck, everything else in fabricating this member is just trimming and shaping in toward a final form, with considerable freedom and forgiveness in the result. Have courage; they make blocks of wood every day.

You need a block of wood, at least four inches long, two inches by three inches in section. Any clear hardwood will do, but the coaming will look best if the apex is of the same stock as the side and back pieces—though I did once use a piece of northern cherry with stunning effect against the rest of the coaming, which was of dark mahogany. An equally good, contrasting combination would be light ash side and back pieces against an apex of black walnut.

Using the width of the block for your siding, make a wedge of your wood block. This is to say, orient the narrowest section forward and aft, and take the wedge scraps off the sides to make a wedge of the same acute angle as the vertical gap between the forward ends of the side pieces (Figure 7–8c). Be conservative; remove only enough wood to allow the wedge to slip down into the gap, the wedge tip just reaching the bottom edge of the side pieces. Then, with the wedge made snug in the gap, use the outside end edge of the side pieces to pencil-mark the rabbet line. On the top of the block mark the approximate angle the rabbet must take. Return the block to the bench and, with a backsaw, a bullnose or rabbet plane, and some chisels, cut out the rabbets. Again, be conservative. Return the block to the boat often to check, recheck, and double-check the correctness of your progress. The reason for the

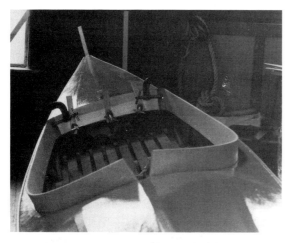

Figures 7-8A-D. Coamings ready for apex or king-piece, sawing out the block from roundstock, establishing the wedge, and looking at the finished piece installed. PHOTO 7-8C BY RICK STAFFORD.

extra length of the wood block is to allow some margin of error during this stage, but the margin is only as good as the wedge is long, and still some extra margin must be saved to allow for rounding over the forward edge of the piece and for a good snug fit into the gap.

Once you have achieved a fair and tight fit, mark with a pencil the top and bottom cut lines and the lines to which you must plane the inside block surface for a perfect fairing into the side pieces. Cut and plane to near these lines; then, with rasp and coarse sandpapers, finish to a good working surface. Predrill, glue, and mount your apex piece (Figure 7–8d). When the glue has set and cured, give the piece the final shape you want and fair it into the side pieces with fine rasp and sandpapers, just as you did on the triangular corner fill pieces.

Give the whole coaming a gentle finish-sanding, using sandpaper of up to #100 grit.

VARNISH

Everyone admires well-varnished brightwork. Almost no one likes to take care of it. Failed varnishwork looks very bad. A boat that looks bad does not generally receive proper care and maintenance. An unmaintained boat gives small pleasure and dies prematurely. Do a really good job on the initial varnish work; if at all possible store the kayak indoors; promptly touch up distressed places when damage occurs, and thoroughly renew the brightwork at the beginning of each boating season. Thus hypocrisy lives. . . .

It takes several days to properly apply varnish—four coats minimum with eight much better—so if you will be using the shop to make the paddle while the various coats of varnish set and dry, you will want to remove the boat to a place where dust and other atmospheric hazards won't damage the finish. A garage, shed, even the outdoors is better than an active woodworking shop.

Both urethane and Varathane exterior varnishes are perfectly acceptable. Choose one with UV absorbers mixed in (pigment added to the varnish to absorb damaging ultraviolet rays), and follow precisely the directions for application, between-coat treatments, and maintenance. The classic surface for these boats, however, is spar (also called marine) varnish with UV absorbers. Used chilled or non-chilled, worked with wet-or-dry or plain dry sandpapers, high-quality spar varnish takes on depth and brilliance. You can achieve similar results with several but not all types of synthetic varnishes. Avoid epoxy and alkyd resins—their maintenance demands limit their practicality. Pure phenolic resin is top-of-the-line synthetic resin; it does not check or crack. You can also use modified phenolics and conventional and aliphatic-modified polyurethanes. The important thing to remember is to use natural solvents (i.e., thinners) with natural varnishes and synthetic (i.e., petroleum-based such as steam-distilled mineral spirits) ones with synthetic varnishes.

Regardless of your choice of varnish, you will need skill and luck to apply it well. The goods news is that the long, narrow finish-woodwork members on this boat forgive imperfect varnishing, even as they reward varnishing of any kind. The big nemesis here is dripping. Do not overfill your brush, and do not flow on the varnish as is recommended for large, flat, bright surfaces. All along the rails, for instance, there are tiny crevices between the wood and the deck canvas overlap that have an insidious way of collecting and holding varnish just long enough for you to turn your back or leave the shop before they release drips that terrify your nicely painted topside or deck. Apply at least four coats. Be frugal, and good luck.

Oh yes, and one other thing . . . I don't know whether you've noticed or not, but if you have gotten this far along in the project, your boat is done. Congratulations, and fair winds to you!

PADDLES AND OARS

There are many possible ways to make a satisfactory kayak double paddle. A very easy and satisfactory method (not illustrated here) is to rip a seven-foot length of spruce 2 × 4 in half; create one-foot-long, ¼-inch slots at both ends of the stock, and into these insert two-foot-long paddle blades made of ¼-inch plywood. Predrill holes at right angles to the slots for bolts or rivets through the blades, set the blades in glue and fasten with at least three fasteners (screws) at both ends. When the glue has set and cured, use spokeshaves, drawknives, planes, rasps and sandpapers to round over and fair the loom (handle) and paddle blades. The blades can be oriented either parallel or at right angles to one another. In either case, several good coats of varnish should be applied to seal the wood, especially the plywood blades. I know several kayakers who have used such paddles for years with great success.

My own preference is to build a fancier paddle for these boats. You have gone to all the work of building your boat—why stint now?

The phrase, "Different strokes for different folks," you may be surprised to learn, originally derived from canoeing, and can be applied for kayaking and rowing as well. Just as you choose different kinds of boats for various uses, so your paddle should be specified for the use you intend. Since the kayaks that emerge from this book are intended for use on large bodies of open, relatively placid water, the paddle I recommend and describe here is also designed and built for such use. It is a relatively long paddle with moderate "whip" and a balanced heft that makes it appropriate for straight passages and for cruising.

The blank from which to shape this paddle is made up of a seven-foot length of hardwood, usually white ash, 2 inches by 1 ½ inches in section, to which two blade blanks of 2-inch pine stock are scarfed. Make the scarf surfaces as long as possible, about seven-to-one (7:1), and glue them with epoxy, clamping them firmly. The shape of the paddle blank(s) is entirely a matter of preference. Some paddlers like spoon-shaped paddles with squared tips. I like a canoe paddle form, and indeed trace onto my blade stock from a 100-year-old, classic canoe paddle made of white maple. If you have built the 18 ½-foot (or larger) kayak or a 17-footer with a long cockpit that can accommodate two paddlers, get out and glue up two paddle blanks. Study the Figure 7–9 photo sequence to see the straightforward procedure I use.

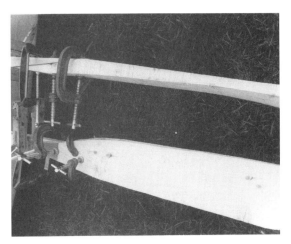

Figures 7-9A-E. Tracing the paddle pattern—itself traced off a canoe paddle I like—paddle blank glued up, oar blank glued up, planing the blades, and spokeshaving the blade/loom scarf.

Once the glue has set and cured, go to work with drawknife and spokeshave on the areas around the scarfs until they fair together in a pleasing way. Then, with planes and sanders, remove excess wood from the blades. This is best done in stages, moving from side to side of each paddle surface at both ends of the paddle, until the blades approach the finish thickness you want. A lot of shaping is involved and the work can become arduous, so don't be in a hurry. Be systematic. Work so that each paddle surface is caught up to the others in section and form as you alternate working surfaces. Take regular breaks from the duty, remembering that fatigued craftsmen make mistakes. When the blades reach the shape you want—fairly thin-edged, graceful yet sturdy, delay their final finish until after the loom (the handle) has been rounded over and faired. Finally, regard the double paddle as a whole. With light shavings and sanding, fair and smooth the entire unit into a flowing, sculptured piece. Remember too our adage: More wood can always be removed. Fortunately, the tendency among novice paddlemakers is to become nervous and leave too much wood, yielding a heavy, stiff paddle. No matter, though, since such pieces can be reworked, lightened, and enlivened with further shaving and refinishing.

Figure 7-10. Finished paddles and oars.

Wood and Canvas Kayak Building

A spoon shape to the blades is rendered by first removing most of the waste wood from the middle portion of one side of the blade blanks and from the end and tip areas on the opposite side. Once you have roughed out the gross spoon form you want, you can finish out the blades as before. However, if your double paddle has blades oriented 90 degrees to each other, before roughing out the opposing blades spoon heft your paddle blank and do a dry-run of the twist you put on the paddle as you alternate strokes from side to side. Spooning the wrong side of a blade can ruin your whole day.

Oars, or more properly sculls, are fabricated using the same methods, but they are rendered as oars. These must come in pairs, are longer (nine feet is common) than paddles, have grips at the inboard ends, are fitted with leathers on the loom, and almost always are terminated in rather broad, square-ended, spooned blades. Their use in these kayaks requires the installation of a rowing unit, and so a cockpit large enough to accommodate one. Various units are available, and you should build your cockpit to the specifications their manufacturer prescribes. (See Appendix B for sources of rowing units.)

Figure 7-11. Kayak fitted with a rowing unit and sculls.

Figures 7-12A-B. The finished boat.

Varnish your paddle(s) to the standard you exercised for your kayak's finish woodwork—or preferably better. After all, paddles are a high visibility item.

Buy champagne, invite friends, and have a name in mind, 'cause it's launch time!

Launching and Using Your Kayak / Diseases, Mishaps, and Repairs

8

The kayak that you have built is not just a thing. As you will discover over time and with use of the boat, it is a craft with a personality and with which you can develop a personal relationship all out of proportion to what its status as a physical object could either account for or justify. With no mysticism implied, good boats become friends. All mariners from all traditions, certainly including Eskimo traditions, have experienced this from time immemorial. Therefore a good boat deserves a name and a ritual at its launching.

LAUNCHING

The commissioning of a new boat is a joyful occasion. It is an optimistic act that should be festively shared with family and friends. Have plenty of food and beverage on hand, and make sure the shoreside bonfire is downwind of the boat. Let there be speeches, toasts, and prayers. When the time comes, invite a young person of choice over to the boat, whisper the name of the boat into her (or his) ear, and have her (him) say aloud to the assembled and to the kayak, "I commission (or launch) thee (name of the boat)," forthwith spilling a dollop of beverage over the forepeak of the boat. The traditional champagne bottle smashed on the bow of boats made of harder material is not appropriate for canvas-covered craft.

To the enthusiastic din of whoops, whistles, and applause, pick up your kayak and wade out into a few inches of water. Assuming a beach launch (rather than a launch from a dock or float), set the boat down so that all but a few inches of the forward bottom floats. Avoid scrapes

Figure 8-1. A launching demands some ceremony, but in the case of canvas-covered craft spill some of the contents over the forepeak instead of smashing the bottle itself on the bow.

and bumps to your kayak. Try to limit unavoidable scraping to the keel. Experienced kayak users generally poke their craft into the water—that is, get into the boat and away from the land as quickly as possible. If you think of your craft as loving the water and hating the land, you will develop the correct launch attitude. Too, kayaks reward cleanliness. Make sure that your feet or soft shoes are free of mud, sand, and grit.

You don't just board a kayak. You have to insert yourself into it, and doing this gracefully with dispatch takes practice. The usual procedure is to lean over, bear down on the boat with hands placed on the gunwales or coaming, and then quickly bring first one leg and then the other up between the arms and into the boat. Larger, less agile paddlers soon discover other means of entry—not without nervousness the first few times. Having friends hold the kayak steady helps a lot. Once in the boat, have assistants push you off, or bear down on the bottom with your paddle to pry the craft free of the shore. You are now afloat and away.

USING YOUR KAYAK

It is not within the purview of this book to instruct on kayaking technique. There are several excellent books on the subject available, and I commend some of them to you in the next chapter. Read at least

Wood and Canvas Kayak Building

one of them. If you are new to this wonderful sport, and this launching is your first experience with a kayak, keep these two things in mind:

Figure 8-2. Pick up your kayak and poke it into the water.

- First, develop a feel for your kayak. Challenge yourself and the boat by tipping her to either side as far over as you dare. Paddle hard and fast, first on one side and then the other. Use the wakes of passing boats to practice handling the kayak in waves—on the bow, the stern, from oblique angles—but try to avoid taking any waves on the beam until you are a proficient paddler. Learn to regard the boat and paddle as part of yourself. You soon will find that the paddle becomes a powerful extension of your arms, giving tremendous bearing to the water as you orient, propel, and maneuver the craft. As you gain skill and confidence the boat almost seems to dissolve and—as motorcyclists, race car drivers, downhill skiers, and figure skaters witness for their sports—the equipment melds with your will, creating a singular and exhilarating experience of just you in motion through the environment.
- Second, safety, safety, and also, safety! Wear and carry all safety equipment required by law. Modern life jackets are much improved over the cork-and-foam life jackets of old, fit well to the body, and do not encumber paddling. Make sure that the one you choose, purchase, and wear carries U.S.C.G.-approved certification right on the jacket. It doesn't hurt to have on board one or two standard size, float cushions with straps. They fit nicely in between floor timbers

forward and aft of the sole, are there for emergencies, and provide comfortable seating, a backrest, and improved survey of the passing scene on leisurely expeditions in placid waters. It is a good idea to equip your life jacket with a police-style whistle, made of either plastic or stainless steel and attached by a plastic lanyard, and light-reflective, waterproof tape across the upper front and back. Another useful item to have on board is a large natural sponge. You will seldom need it, but in the event of a leak or troublesome wave splash and spray, a large sponge will clear a kayak of water with surprising efficiency.

For true safety, nothing, no *thing* replaces skill and competence with your boat and good seamanship. You have no radio aboard. You cannot call for help beyond the sound of your voice or whistle, and being seen in trouble is strictly a matter of luck, on which only fools depend. Anticipate trouble; then work to prevent it by becoming a good kayaker. Be very timid at first. Then go through intrepid exercises inshore, in shallow water. Roll the boat over and fill it—it won't sink. Practice hanging onto the boat and swimming alongside of it. Grasp the coaming and rock the boat, spilling and splashing water out of it until it regains some stability, providing a more visible and movable platform. Practice getting out of and then back into a partially filled boat. You cannot love or enjoy a boat that frightens you!

Figure 8-3. Develop a feel for your kayak so that you can regard boat and paddle as part of yourself—or in this instance, yourselves.

Wood and Canvas Kayak Building

In regard to the United States Coast Guard and other safety regulatory agencies, do not depend on them for your safety. They will not be there when you get into trouble, and you should not expect them to be. When they do discover you, participate fully in all of their requests, and answer all their questions forthrightly. As a rule, people generally, and safety officials specifically, do not understand kayaks and kayakers; in fact they do not believe that safe conduct in a kayak is a possibility. In addition to maintaining aids to navigation, responding to distress calls, and enforcing marine, immigration, and drug laws, these men and women also have to deal with many, very stupid, incompetent people on the water—dealings that include removing their dead bodies and unfortunate boats from the scene of accidents. When Coast Guard officials stop you for a safety check, they are neither in the mood nor in a disposition to listen to a lecture on the viability and safety of your craft. Do not lecture them. They think that kayakers are crazy. Only we know that we are not. Forgive them their doubts and cooperate completely. And practice, study to become a good paddler.

The Rowing Option

Those interested in the rowing potential of larger versions of these kayaks will find rowing machines available that will fit snugly into the

Figure 8-4. With some modifications (see the text) in the Oarmaster rowing unit, this boat goes like blazes using the oars shown in production in Chapter 7.

cockpit. (See Appendix B for sources.) The Charles River Oarmaster shown here is an excellent kit that, with no adjustments, drops into appropriately specified cockpits just fine. It was obtained from Martin Marine, whose literature provides complete details on the Oarmaster's dimensions, and on the company's excellent line of rowing accoutrements, including oars. In the kayak in Figure 8–4, I reduced the depth of the wooden uprights on the sliding seat by 2 ½ inches, lowering the center of gravity in the boat, but also raising the level at which the rower grips the oars. The result was entirely satisfactory. The boat goes like blazes with the 9 ½-foot oars shown in production (see Chapter 7), and yet retains all the other features and flexibility of a large family kayak.

KAYAK DISEASES, MISHAPS, AND REPAIRS

Canvas can be punctured, chafed, torn, and ripped. It also mildews and rots. The woodwork can be chafed, strained, and broken. It also can rot. Fastenings can corrode, stain through the canvas, and come unfastened. Glue can come unstuck. Eventually some of these problems are going to occur to your kayak. It is nobody's fault. You could have begun to collect milk glass instead of building a canvas-covered kayak and avoided these difficulties. In any case, if not catastrophically extensive, the problems can be fixed.

The most common disease of canvas boats is pollution. Small chips of wood, lost fastenings, and even sanding sawdust collected in the boat while under construction can cause problems early in the boat's career. Later on, mud, sand, gravel, and small stones brought aboard by paddlers become lodged between stringers and chines and the skin to begin their insidious work. Anything that gets between the framework and the canvas creates a protuberance, cracks the paint, raises the canvas, and presents a chafing surface that soon breeches the skin and leaks. Vigilance will spot these things, and they can be dislodged by drumming on the bottom of the boat with your hands, setting up a rhythm that sends waves through the canvas and eventually loosens and frees the offender. When, for whatever reason, small holes do appear over parts of the frame, the cure is to carefully tease out the threads around the hole with the point of your dividers (a pen knife will do) and dab epoxy into and around the puncture. Paint over the wound after the glue has cured.

Large holes, tears, and rips not backed by wood members naturally give more trouble. Unless the tear is reachable by hand from the inside, attempts at sewing the canvas (with a sailmaker's cross-stitch) will not

Figure 8-5. A veteran of many repairs. The sail tape showing here is three seasons old and needs replacing—ripping up, the substrate scuffed up, new tape applied, and repainting.

be successful. The best solution is to gently but thoroughly scuff the paint around the offending hole or rip, and cover to it with sail repair tape, being particularly generous with the tape at either end of tears (across the canvas stitching) and rips (along the stitching). Make absolutely sure that the repair tape makes a good seal all around its edge. The few times that I have had to do this I've gone around the edge of the tape with a prime of clear bathtub caulk, which I applied and smoothed off the end of a finger. Rubber cement of the kind that comes with auto inner-tube repair kits, or plastic model cement (the kind used in model airplane making) also would work. Once you have sealed the repair by whatever method you elect, prime and paint over the bandage. Since it is nearly impossible to duplicate the color of older paint, the cosmetic problems of the repair can sometimes be ameliorated by owning up to the problem with a contrasting paint in some sort of figure—a fish, dolphin, sea bird . . . whatever fancies or seems appropriate.

Rot and breakage are different matters. They require surgery. But it is not so cataclysmic as you may think, for paint-soaked canvas has good "memory"—that is, it goes back into position easily—and major repairs usually require no more than a few days in the shop.

Almost always you have to get under the deck canvas. To do this, use a small screwdriver to score out the plastic wood from the countersinks along the rail on the side of the boat where the problem lies. Back out all of the screws and remove the rail. Then, again with a small

Figure 8-6. Up comes the deck canvas on a much-repaired old kayak. Note my early use of staples and how the canvas was crimped over the top of the gunnel strips—neither a current practice. The ratty looking deck stringer went in several years ago as an emergency repair, as did the cockpit carlins, which were rockers from a junked rocking chair. Not only did the repair work well, but waste not, want not.

screwdriver or tack remover, pop out all of the copper tacks that hold the deck canvas to the gunwales. This will give you access to the interior of the hull.

Breaks in the framework are repaired the same way that doctors repair bone fractures—by resetting the pieces in position, and reinforcing the traumatized area. Smear epoxy generously into the breaks and reset the piece(s) into proper position. Then, "sister" the broken area—that is, take a length of stock the same dimension as the broken member (usually strip stock), cut it to a length that overlaps the break by at least three inches at either end, smear its bearing surface with epoxy, and push it into position over the stressed place. If the skin prevents you from using clamps, then rig some sort of thrusting setup that holds the sister piece in position while the glue sets and cures. With systematic diagnosis and procedure, even extensive and complicated traumas to the framework can be repaired in this way. Complete disasters are, I'm afraid, complete.

When and while you have the boat opened up, use the opportunity to examine the entire inside structure and inner skin surface of the boat. Any weakened areas in the woodwork should be reinforced by sistering, as described above. Once in a while, after several years, some of the normal mildew spots that develop on the inside surface of the canvas will locally weaken the canvas fabric. These places should be brushed sparingly with canvas preservative (available from awning suppliers and good chandlers) or with your own mix of kerosene, turpentine, and mildew disinfectant (available at good hardware stores). I have never dared to use canvas preservative treatments on new boat skins, because the ones I know about are not compatible with the paints I use. The chemists have been busy and found a way, so if you are using different paints from the ones I have recommended, or if you are interested in pursuing the possibility of treating new canvas skin, consult a reputable paint/preservative dealer or, better though less immediate, the manufacturers of the products you want to use. The possible combinations are too numerous to be addressed in this book.

When your examination and repairs are completed, reaffix the deck canvas. If the original tacks are sound, it is OK to use the same ones, in the same holes as before. Remount the rail, apply plastic wood to the countersinks, sand smooth, and varnish.

Figure 8-7. A weak place in the bottom stringers sistered years ago with good results.

Cracks in the paint become problematical after a few years, especially if you store the craft outdoors where the elements, particularly sunlight, get to it. Store the boat indoors or under cover as much as possible. When cracks do accumulate, buff them with #80-grit sandpaper and prime them with thinned urethane paint before applying your color coat over the whole craft.

Figures 8-8A-B. A close-up of the inside surface of eight-year-old canvas. What you see is rust and mildew stains and the impact zones where paint on the outside has cracked, subsequent paintings penetrating these cracks and resealing the skin. While still serviceable, the old skin was removed from the framework for general overhaul work.

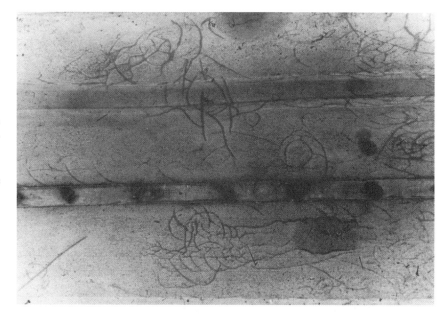

Wood and Canvas Kayak Building

Figure 8-9. Copper nails driven down through the coaming to keep grain from "chasing" and to prevent breakage when the paddlers bear down on it while getting in and out of the boat. Placing hands on the gunwales is preferable.

All canvas boats sooner or later begin to leak a little bit. All kayaks get water into them through ordinary use. Large amounts of water can be evacuated through the cockpit aperture by turning the boat upside down and rocking it from side to side. Small amounts can be removed with a sponge. A dry boat is a happier boat, but since canvas kayaks are fated to be often damp, the rules of thumb are:

- Keep the boat as water-free as possible, as much as possible. Salt water is less harmful than fresh water.
- When ambient water in the boat becomes a problem, install a drain hole through the head of one of the stem timbers. This is done by drilling a ¼-inch hole at an angle through the canvas and into the boat through the top of a stem timber. This hole should be either dressed with a sail grommet sized to the ¼-inch hole, glued, and tapped into position, or it can be lined with a short length of copper tubing set in glue. You can then drain the boat regularly by storing it with this end downward. Be sure to clear the drain hole of any obstructions each time you store the craft.

It is the cockpit that receives human traffic and abuse. Broken sections of coaming are repaired by edge-gluing the piece back into place. You then drill downward from the top through the broken piece well into the sound coaming wood below. Drive copper nails of appropriate number (every 1 ½ inches) and length into these holes. Dress the nail heads with a file and countersink them very slightly with a punch. Sand smooth the distressed area and varnish.

Finally, a general guideline: Canvas kayaks are much tougher than common sense would assume. Think of the boat as a dear piece of equipment, like a fine sports car or camera. Take it out and let it do its stuff, but then take care of it, as it so graciously serves you.

Final Remarks

9

The kayak presented in this book is of ancient design and rendered in old-fashioned, occidental construction. Throughout the course of construction I have offered freedom and choice in design detail, and alternative ways to handle particular building procedures. Some people are uncomfortable with such direction, and prefer recipes with explicit instructions, unembellished by choices and the need to make decisions. To these folk I apologize. For everyone I provide in Appendix A the original article by Norman Skene, which, in few words, describes the boat as originally presented in *The Rudder* magazine of June, 1923. This article launched a veritable host of kayaks over the ensuing 40 years, and was the basis of the early craft built in my shop, and so eventually of this book.

EXTRAPOLATING OPTIONS AND ALTERNATIVES

As I said in the first chapter, these kayaks are basically bridges with canvas skins stretched over them. A little extrapolation quickly leads to the thought that many other kinds of boats, with differing proportions and other kinds of materials, also could be made using this system of construction. Absolutely correct!

A friend of mine skinned his kayak frame in fiberglass cloth and resin, and did not bother to install a deck. He used it as a canoe on Penobscot Bay for several years with entire success. Except for a bit of "scalloping," where the fiberglass cured to a slight concavity between longitudinal members, the hull looked fine. Since he did not use

Figure 9-1. Skene's
original article (see
Appendix A) was the
basis of the early craft
built in my workshop—
indeed of many such
craft—and eventually of
this book.

pigment in the fiberglass matrix, sunlight showed through the hull,
setting off the framework and making an intriguing sight!

Other high-tech, skinning system options are carbon-fiber–reinforced Kevlar set in resin or aircraft-quality, heat-shrunk Dacron
cloth set in butanol paint or plastic resins. These provide very tough,
ultralight hull structures, at considerable added cost.

More traditionally, you could use shellac-soaked paper. Paper
canoes enjoyed considerable vogue a hundred years ago. It is simply a
matter of building up a papier mache with shellac or some other
binder. A boatbuilder acquaintance of mine once experimented, laying
up only three layers of regular, grocery bag paper in resin. The resulting
sheet withstood repeated blows with a sledgehammer. It bent but did
not break. In any case, Nathaniel Bishop's famous book, *Voyage of the
Paper Canoe,* and its sequels that describe adventures on America's
inland rivers in paper-and-shellac boats during the late 19th century,
can still be found in libraries and secondhand book stores, and are
inspirational reading, indeed!

Too, there is no reason why these boats could not be sheathed in
wood, strip-built of edge-glued strips or veneers using the old Ashcraft
system, modern composite systems (including the WEST system), or
the system that has become popular among "backyard" boatbuilders
in England, called the CABBS system (a stitch-and-glue system). The
latter is a very simple method suitable for many boats with hard chines.
Full-sized panels of ⅛- or ³⁄₁₆-inch plywood are cut to fit the sides and
two halves of the bottom. These are lightly pinned to the gunwales,

chines, and keelson to hold them in place while small holes are drilled along the panel-to-panel joints. These holes are stitched with copper wire that is woven down the line of adjoining holes. The whole is then sheathed in fiberglass and sanded smooth, yielding what in essence is a bright finish.

Another fascinating, and not necessarily a fantasy, notion is to power one of these boats. If wood sheathing were employed, and the boat given a vertical stern piece and deadwood skeg, the boat could be tapped for a shaft and small propeller. A ½ h.p. electric motor run from two heavy-duty marine batteries, controlled by a hand-operated rheostat, would make for a splendid "sneakboat," one that would be fast enough and good for several hours of silent travel in nature-watching and photography. The batteries could be stowed forward and aft of the cockpit, each with its own hatch for removal, recharging, and maintenance. Can you see it? Moving along at an even speed, silently, through rafts of waterfowl, your eyes and camera just peeking over the coaming, your feet steering the craft through a quadrant over the rudder at the stern.

Such dreams!

That is why I have written this book with so many options and choices. You do not set out to build a boat because either the building or the boat is practical. You do it because the activity itself is pleasurable, and in the doing you make yourself and your life better. The boat is a bonus. Enjoy it to the fullest.

SOME HELPFUL BOOKS

So-called how-to books are a staple in the publishing industry. Thousands of new titles appear every year, even as thousands go out of print into obscurities more or less deserved. This abundance of craft-method books is unique to our times; in most times past particular crafts were the exclusive preserve of guildsmen, tradesmen, and particular classes or life stations. Today we are a wonderfully privileged people in our social and informational access to the world's craft knowledge at a time when the experts can tell what they know with impunity. From the plethora of possibilities I suggest here a few books that will make your craftsmanship and kayaking better.

Woodworking Technique

Woodworking is the epitome of American craftsmanship. To a land of diverse and abundant raw material, English, German, and Scandinavian settlers brought the best elements of European woodcrafts. Knowledge of these techniques became an American legacy. Unfortunately this legacy was undermined by a major depression, a world war, and a glorification of the "instant" benefits that industry offered an expanding middle class. The latter force especially rendered genuine woodcraft quaintly obsolete and embarrassing.

Then history threw one of those what-goes-around-comes-around tricks in the late 1960s, and interest in rediscovering and preserving traditional craftsmanship grew at a rapid pace. There emerged a critical mass—enough people to create general interest and a demand market for the information, materials, and tools to practice virtually all of the ancient crafts, woodworking prominent among them.

Sniffing a change in the wind, Woodcraft Supply (then of Boston, now of Woburn, Massachusetts), began to advertise their wares. For years a supplier of fine European and English woodworking tools to specialty wood artisans, this shop came "out of the woodwork" in 1971, becoming the vanguard to the rebirth of American woodcrafts. Many other outfits soon followed suit, splendid magazines such as *WoodenBoat* and *Fine Woodworking* appeared, and all around the country forestry and USDA Extension agents were being asked the way to reliable sawyers and suppliers. Oddly enough, the very first book that Woodcraft Supply offered in those limited and gratefully gone days—the only good book on the topic available anywhere at the time—remains in my mind one of the best available today.

This is *Planecraft: Handplaning by Modern Methods,* by C.W. Hampton and E. Clifford (Woodcraft Supply; Woburn, MA, 1982). Written 60 years ago under the auspices of the Record Tool Company of England for woodworking apprentices, this book is not exciting. This book is adventure in sequential simple declarative sentences. This book is clear. This book will change your life! In the process of describing methods and techniques of sharpening, setting, and using planes and their close cousins (spokeshaves, scrapers, etc.), the book forces the reader to absorb a philosophy that will pervade all shop practices, and much life practice beyond the shop. Here without self-consciousness or embarrassment is Man (Person) the Tool-User, whose usual relationship with the world, with materials, is through the use of tools. Three-quarters of the tools in a woodworking shop work by cutting. This book is the how, why, and wherefore of cutting, the primary means by which trees become manufactured effects. Even if your only tool is a pocket knife, you should read this book. Other than this one, there are these days a hundred marvelous good books in print on tools and woodworking, and I commend all of them to you.

General Watercraft History

Neither in the first chapter nor here will I indulge a thesis about skin boats being Man's First Watercraft or any similar paleo-maritime nonsense. In fact, you will do the marine publishing industry a service by formally objecting to all published speculation about Homo sapiens' (or any other hominid's) first impulses to go to sea via anything other than his or her own subcutaneous adipose tissue (fat) or a truly viable craft of some kind. It's incredible that even some respectable marine historians have published illustrations of a cave man on a log with a caption reading something like "Man's First Boat." The authors and editors of such books have never tried a log. If they had, they would have rejected it just as readily and vituperatively as early peoples regularly did whenever desperation or idiocy compelled them to try it. Except when lashed into rafts, logs don't work. They aren't boats and there is no evidence of their being either used or considered as such, therefore scholars have no business perpetrating the notion in the first place!

Hollowed-out logs, however, are boats, and so are any framework constructions that are woven with rushes or covered by leathers (or any other material), and so launched on waters for transport of any kind. Where trees are large and wood is plentiful, wood is used exclusively. Where trees are small and wood is dear, skin-covered framework boats are developed, especially by peoples with access to large animals with thick, tough hides. Unfortunately, published scholarship about the geography, history, and technology of skin-covered craft is very scanty, even if excellent. What little there is devoted mostly to circumarctic Inuit (Eskimo) examples. Brief references here and there in the anthropological literature from north and east Africa, India, and central North America (e.g., Mandan Indians on the Missouri River), are as intriguing as they are frustrating.

One rather modest exception is *The Curraghs of Ireland*, by James Hornell (The Society for Nautical Research, Greenwich, England, 1973). This is a collection of articles, which originally were published in *The Mariner's Mirror* during the 1930s. The articles circumnavigate Ireland in word and (badly reproduced) photographs, documenting the construction and use of the (nearly) last generation of canvas-covered, skin boats to be used in the folk fisheries and transport of the maritime Irish. This very ancient boat type derives from forebears covered with ox hides, and its traditions benefit from the legends of Saints Columbo, Patrick, and especially Brendan. Curraghs are wonderful boats, extremely able and still in service in the west of Ireland. Figures

Figure 9-2. Bending a kayak rib without steaming; from David Zimmerly's *The Acquisition and Documentation of an Artifact*.

1–2 and 1–3 in Chapter 1 show three-station curraghs in 1970 meeting a ferry boat to liter passengers and cargo to Inishsheer, Aran Islands, which has neither harbor nor water depth sufficient to accommodate the ferry from Galway. Hornell and the Society also published an accompanying pamphlet on the coracles (wicker-framed, round, skin-covered craft mostly used on rivers) of Britain and Wales.

The rest of the literature looks to high latitudes, and, though few in number, the books that deal directly and exclusively with kayaks and related craft are first-rate.

The granddaddy text is *The Bark Canoes and Skin Boats of North America,* by Edwin Tappan Adney and Howard I. Chapelle (Smithsonian Institution, Washington, D.C., 1964). Since it came out this book has been the basic text from which most subsequent discussions about native craft in North America derive. The relatively late publishing date of the book clouds the fact that Chapelle's interest in the field, and most of his contributions to the text, were generated about the time of the First World War. Indeed, the Norman Skene design of *Walrus,* to which this book is devoted, was based on Chapelle's early research and lines that later appeared in the Smithsonian volume. Any basic, skin boat, library collection begins with this book.

Before I bibliograph kayaks specifically, readers interested in the larger, open, Arctic skin boats—umiaks, angyapiks, and their ilk—

should get hold of *The Skin Boats of Saint Lawrence Island, Alaska*, by Stephen R. Braund (University of Washington Press, Seattle and London, 1988). This surprisingly complete and heavily illustrated book exceeds its scholarly purpose and could be downright inspirational to anyone with a mind to explore the possibilities of skin-covered technology for larger nautical craft.

Kayak-Specific Books

Now then, kayaks: In regards to kayak lore, ethnology, and construction, two authors have the field covered like a blanket. They are almost miraculously good, especially considering how many fields of very specialized interest have scores of authors, none of whom are distinguished. Our heros are David Zimmerly and George Dyson.

David Zimmerly is one of those ''students of people'' who prefer being in the field to being in the offices of the institutions that support their scholarship. For years associated with the Museum of Man, recently become the Museum of Civilization in Ottawa, Ontario, Canada, Zimmerly is a hard man to find. More often than not he has ingratiated himself to a very old, native, kayak builder and won for himself a patch of cabin floor that he will call home for months at a time as he discovers and records moment by moment, action by action, every step and aspect of indigenous kayak construction. Nearly two decades ago David Zimmerly recognized 16 basic circumarctic kayak types and determined that he would research and record all of them in their most pristine traditions while the last of the traditional builders and users remained alive to show and tell. The man is clearly, wonderfully nuts. He is still out there doing it, half-done during the eleventh hour. He will never be done. It is nearly midnight. . . .

Two Zimmerly publications that directly apply to our project in this book are *An Illustrated Glossary of Kayak Terminology* and *The Acquisition and Documentation of an Artifact*, the latter publication recording not only the design and construction of a native Alaskan kayak, but then replicating the boat in occidental, canvas-covered construction using methods very similar to those employed in our project here. Zimmerly's documented and published material goes far beyond these recommended works, including sets of full-scale lines and parts pattern drawings for specific, Alaskan kayak types.

As for George Bernard Dyson, his book, *Baidarka* (Alaska Northwest Publishing Company, Edmonds, Washington, 1988), is the best book on kayaks as artifacts ever written—so good that it must be considered a seminal, virtually immortal work in the field. Go to your

Figure 9-3. The cover to
An Illustrated Glossary of Kayak Terminology.

Figure 9-4. The cover to
Baidarka.

local bookstore and order it now. Read it. Cherish it. Read it again. Show it to others. My attitude toward Dyson's book would be the same even if its purposes were the same as this book's. As it is, the orientation and purposes are complementary because in some ways they are so much more advanced. After thoroughly documenting the history and technology of the general baidarka type of Alaskan kayak, the author then records the building of several, including a monster with six stations and three sails! Especially interesting is the last section of the book that describes an ultra-high-tech, two-station version of the boat, using welded aluminum sections and tube stringers, all skinned with double-woven, two-ply nylon fabric, yielding what is no doubt the most powerful kayak ever built. Eccentric, compelling, stimulating, wonderful reading and reference.

The early European penetrators of North America, most notoriously the missionaries, trappers, and voyageurs, used native-built, and later native-inspired, canoes and boats as a matter of course. Rough and rugged men, isolated by their wilderness environment and remoteness from their own cultural origins (and not seldom alienated by the criminal intentions of their patrons), the advantageous aspects of the boats they used in the vast New World trading network were slow to advertisement in England and Europe. Gradually, though, word and examples of the craft were smuggled or otherwise sent to the homelands for eventual recognition by a growing middle class, which had waiting discretionary funds and extra time on its hands for sport—sports like canoeing!

It took the emerging middle class of Victorian England to adopt and adapt the exotic native North American models to their own purposes and pleasures. Foremost among the early popularizers of recreational canoeing, in decked, very kayak-like craft, was John MacGregor, a barrister-at-law, who made a series of extraordinary cruises in small, decked canoes on the lakes and rivers of Europe and in the Baltic during the 1870s, 1880s, and 1890s. His books, especially *1000 Miles in a Rob Roy Canoe* (last available from Canoeing Press, Derby, England, currently out of print), became very popular in Britain. Canoeing clubs sprang up everywhere. His personable style, technical discussions, and truly intrepid adventures gave and still give inspiration, courage, excitement, and verve to the prospect of owning and using a small, decked canoe or kayak.

Of course, the English connection soon began to infect American society, and premiere among the names associated with canoeing here was that of Henry Rushton. He served an entire generation of American enthusiasts by manufacturing gorgeous canoes and small boats. During his time few bodies of water in the eastern United States were without their canoeing club. Indeed, in great-great-grandfather's era, roughly 100 years ago, canoeing and rowing had many of the same social status characteristics as do running and aerobics today. It was High Physical Culture, and Rushton's prestigious craft in the movement are all beautifully described in *Rushton and His Times in American Canoeing,* by Atwood Manley (Syracuse University Press, Syracuse, N.Y., 1968). Odd as it may seem, the recreational potential of America's native boat was introduced to us by the English, whom we had renounced subjection to a century before.

My final book recommendations are most important. However you decide to take an interest in and pursue information about small, decked canoes and kayaks as objects of history or pleasure, the time comes when you find yourself on the water in one. Then there is no such thing as too much information! There is only one, really good book about using kayaks of native model on the ocean or other large bodies of water. This is *Sea Kayaking,* by Derek C. Hutchinson (Globe Pequot Press, Chester, CT, 1985). Everything that you can learn from mere words is in this book. It is mandatory. Don't ask questions; just get it, read it. Photocopy pages out of it and tape them to your bathroom mirror; have people you love whisper pages from it, and people you hate scream them at you.

Were this not enough, you really should learn to roll your kayak. There are many different kinds of rolls and special maneuvers, all of which will make your kayaking much more pleasurable, safe, and fulfilling. The definitive, mandatory book on the subject is *Eskimo Rolling,* also by Derek Hutchinson (International Marine Publishing Company, Camden, Maine, 1988).

The reason why so few other books have appeared to compete with the above titles is that these books are so very good. Kayakers constitute a wonderfully special society, and we can all be glad that our craft and paddling have features that can never be sold wholesale to ambitious fools. The authors in the field are serious, and not in it for the money. I consider it an extraordinary privilege to count myself among them with this frankly fraternal, no doubt obscure effort. What is not obscure is that, if you come to build one of these boats, use it, and learn its ways, your relationship with the water will be changed, and so your relationship with yourself and others, forever.

Appendix A
Building Plans of Walrus, Esquimo Kayak

Designed for The Rudder by Norman L. Skene

No. XX in The Rudder's Series of Working Plans

Note—We cannot guarantee safety, speed nor seaworthiness of this boat if built at variance with the drawings and specifications. If changes are contemplated we should be consulted

ABORIGINAL craft are always very interesting, representing as they do the native's solution, arrived at after a period of centuries of development of the problem of a craft exactly suited to his requirements, environment and materials available for construction. The result is always a very practical craft and generally a beautiful one even when measured by civilized standards.

The kayak is an interesting example of savage naval architecture. Built of seal skin stretched over a light wood frame, they are very fine-lined, speedy and fairly seaworthy. In them the Eskimo does his Summer hunting and becomes prodigiously skilful in their use. They are completely decked save for a hole barely large enough for a man to crowd the lower half of his body through. He wears a waterproof skin jacket which he fits outside the coaming and lashes tightly to it, making man and boat a unit, a sort of marine centaur.

Whalers and explorers relate amazing tales of native skill with the kayak—of seeing Eskimos swap canoes at sea, of their turning completely over and righting again at will, and of meeting a heavy breaking sea with this manoeuver; in fact, there are photographs of this accomplishment. Although he cannot swim, the Eskimo ventures many miles from land in his tiny craft and from it harpoons walrus, narwhal and seals. One great advantage of the type is its quick acceleration—its ability to spurt ahead or astern equally well when necessary to avoid the rush of an enraged walrus. The hunter creeps up to within forty feet of the walrus and hurls his harpoon, which is connected by a rawhide line with a float made of the inflated skin of a baby seal. After dispatching the animal, which may weigh over a ton, the hunters tow it to land or an ice flow and cut it up.

Each kayak is built to suit its builder's personal require-ments, making its dimensions and displacement proportionate to his own size. The kayak is about the speediest little craft there is except a rowing shell. A native in a kayak can keep up with an ordinary small power boat for quite a distance. Types vary considerably in different parts of the Arctic. In some sections a very tiny, low-sided kayak is used, in others a larger, more seaworthy model. Both V-bottom and flat-bottom models are used. The lines shown herewith were taken by the writer from kayaks brought from different parts of Greenland and are very good examples.

The sport of kayaking is one with which few people are familiar, but which deserves great popularity. It is the finest kind of athletics, combining vigorous exercise, sea bathing and sun bathing. Clad in an abbreviated bathing suit and equipped with a light double-bladed paddle, one can travel long distances without fatigue in this easily-driven, sporty little craft. An occasional plunge overboard adds to the zest of kayaking. With practice one can climb in again without difficulty.

Walrus is the South Greenland type of kayak. I have modified it principally by increasing the beam three inches and giving it a little less deadrise to increase the stability; also in providing a deck opening easier to get in and out of. These modifications make the boat thoroughly practicable for use by anyone weighing up to 180 lbs. Quite a number of kayaks have been built from this design and wherever they are used they attract a great deal of interest and attention. They are really quite seaworthy and with a little practice one acquires quickly the necessary skill to manage them under any circumstances.

Walrus is 17 feet long, 22 inches wide, weighs 45 pounds, costs about $10.00 for materials, and can be built in about a week. It is about the easiest boat to build you

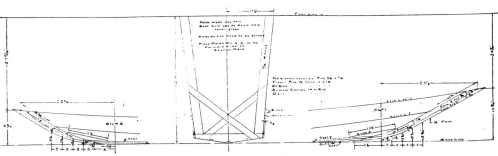

Setting-Up Plan for Walrus

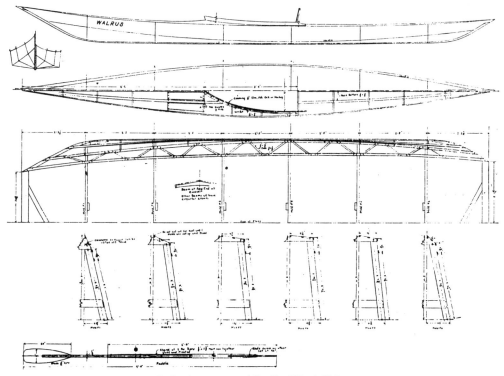

Profile, Arrangement and Details of Kayak Walrus

can imagine, for there is no steam bending, no hardwood except the coaming, and no planking. The construction is the same as the Eskimos use, substituting canvas for seal-skin, stretched over a light wood frame.

The framework, except floors and deck beams, is all one size, ⅜" x ⅞", split from a board of clear spruce, cedar or soft pine. If you are not able to procure an 18-foot board, the longer pieces may be spliced by scarphing and gluing and reinforcing after the stick is bent in place with a short stick fitted on the inside. The inner and outer stems are band-sawed to shape shown on the detail.

The boat is built upside down on a level board floor, as this is the easiest way to set it up perfectly true and to get the bottom canvas on. The exact shape and location of the molds is shown in the drawings. The molds are made to the inside of side stringers, as shown, but the bottom stringers and keel are let in.

First you snap a centerline on the floor, then mark off on it the stations or locations for molds, 2 ft. 5 in. apart. The molds are not beveled, so the forward face of molds 1, 2, 3 are placed on the mark and the after faces of molds 5, 6, 7 on the station marks. The molds are tacked to floor square with centerline and braced to stand plumb and with centers directly over the centerline on the floor. It is not necessary to give instructions of great minuteness, as anyone with any mechanical ability at all will have no difficulty in putting Walrus together in accordance with the plans.

After the molds are in place a little post is set up at each end to locate the stem heads and the stems are set up and kneed to inner keel. These inner stems are not bevelled, being full ⅞" thick all over. The clamps, bilge chines and bottom stringers are now put in place, being tacked to molds and bevelled and screw-fastened to the stems. There is considerable twist to the bottom stringers at the ends, which may be helped by putting the two sticks outdoors for a week before they are needed, fastening the middle third temporarily to something and putting a 90° twist in each end by a lever screwed to it. After a week of this it will retain sufficient twist to be placed easily.

The framework is all put together with brass screws, ¾" No. 3 or ⅞" copper nails clinched. The topside bracing is put in diagonally, as shown, to form a truss and give the boat sufficient longitudinal strength. A cross floor and a deckbeam is fitted at each mold and one between. These may well be a little higher than the longitudinal members, 7/16" or ½".

After the frame is all together, the next operation is to put on the bottom canvas. First draw all the temporary fastenings from the frame into the molds. Be sure to get every one out. Also see that all fastenings are flush, so they will not protrude into the canvas. The canvas used on the bottom is 10 oz. and you will require a piece 3 ft. x 17 ft. The canvas is put on dry, selecting a dry day unless you have a heated shop. Tack the canvas to the

Building Plans of Kayak

(Continued from Page 21)

keel on one end and stretch moderately fore and aft. Then tack all along the keel at about 8" intervals. Slit the canvas back on the center line at each end beyond the curvature of the forefoot as far as the straight of the keel. Then start at one end and tack to the clamp on one side, stretching as tightly as possible. Use small copper tacks driven at 2" intervals. When the canvas is tacked down on both sides full length, you can tack to stems. When one side is tacked, trim it off close to the stem and stretch the other side over it. Put a thick layer of paint between, and trim off this side flush with stem. Be careful to stretch tightly all over. It is not difficult to stretch the canvas if only a little care, muscle and "gumption" is used. Next put on the outer stems and the false keel fastening with screws.

It is easier to fill and paint the bottom now before removing the boat from the molds. Wet the canvas thoroughly with a sponge and paint it immediately while wet, forcing the paint in liberally with a thick brush. Use a heavy deck paint for this purpose and give it two or three coats, as necessary. It will be well to wait until the boat is finished before applying the finishing coat and varnish.

Lift the boat from the molds. Tack a strip across the gunwales amidships first to prevent the boat spreading. You can now fit deck beams and the three longitudinal strips over which the deck canvas is stretched. A thin piece of wood decking is fitted just forward of the cockpit to take the thrust of the paddler's toes, so that we will not press up on the deck canvas. It is a very easy matter to stretch the deck canvas, for which 8 oz. is suitable. If you wish to be real economical you can sew together the trimmings from the bottom canvas, which will be sufficient to cover the after deck and a large part of the fore deck.

Next fit the floor boards, for which 3/16" is thick enough if adequately supported, and get the floor as low as possible in the boat. Fit the carlins next for the coamings. These carlins may be ¾ x ⅞" split vertically for the forward three-fourths of every length to make them bend easily in place. When thru-fastened they will be very rigid. The coamings should be of ¼" oak, elm or mahogany, put in as shown. Fit two pieces of ¾" x 1/16" brass over the points of the stems to protect them.

You are now ready for painting. After filling the deck as described for the bottom, sandpaper the boat down to a smooth surface with fine sandpaper and apply two coats of japan color mixed up with turpentine. Over this two coats of spar varnish will give a very handsome and serviceable finish. One pound of the japan color should be enough. You will need about five quarts of deck paint for the foundation. Two brightly varnished chafing strips are to be fitted along each gunwale.

You are now ready to try her out and I know you will get more fun for your money than you could out of any other boat.

BLOCK ISLAND RACE DATE

In the May number of THE RUDDER we announced the date of the Block Island Race as July 7th. The information received was wrong, as we now find out from Regatta Committee Chairman Walter S. Sullivan, who sends us the correct date as being July 14th.

"Building Plans of *Walrus*, Eskimo Kayak," *The Rudder*, June, 1923

Appendix B

Manufacturers and Suppliers of Materials

Woodcraft Supply Corp., 10 State Street, P.O. Box 4000, Woburn, MA 01888. 617/935-5860; 800/225-1153. Woodcraft publishes the book, **Planecraft** ($6.50). The company also can supply a Kestrel **crooked knife.**

North West Company, Inc., 440 Wyld Street, North Bay, Ontario, P1B 1Z5, Canada. 705/472-6940; 705/472-9380 FAX. This is the firm to contact for the **crooked knife** referred to in the text. Currently the knife is available with handle; North West may again produce the knife blade only. The crooked knife costs $29.98 (Canadian) plus shipping and handling. The company can take Visa/Mastercard orders from the U.S. by phone or FAX.

Canvas Crafts, 501A North Fort Harrison Avenue, Clearwater, FL 34615. 813/447-0189; 800/366-4405. You can get **untreated Midwest duck canvas** or **Canvak pretreated cotton duck canvas** from this company. It also carries **Kevlar, Dacron,** and **Acrylan canvas,** and **Vivatex** and **Permasol** canvas preservatives. The catalog costs $2 (refunded on first order). Company representatives note that the catalog cannot list everything the company carries; if you don't see what you want, ask for it.

Canvas/David Niewolski, 32 Mount Auburn Street, Watertown, MA 02172. 617/926-4353. A complete inventory of **natural, untreated canvas** for decks and canoes.

Aircraft Spruce, Box 424, Fullerton, CA 92632. 714/870-7551. Supplier of **aircraft Dacron.**

Sailrite Kits, 305 West Van Buren Street, P.O. Box 987, Columbia City, IN 46725. 800/348-2769. A good company for **alternative skins**—Acrylan canvas, Dacron, and Kevlar.

Chesapeake Marine Fasteners, P.O. Box 6521, Annapolis, MD 21401. 301/268-8973; 800/526-0658. This company has both sizes of **copper tacks**—⅜-inch for the 17-foot model and ½-inch for the 18 ½-foot version—and ¾-inch #8 **bronze screws**.

Jamestown Distributors, 28 Narragansett Avenue, P.O. Box 348, Jamestown, RI 02835. 401/423-2520 (in RI or outside the U.S.); 800/423-0030 (out-of-state U.S.). **Copper tacks** in ⅜ inch and ½ inch sizes can be purchased from Jamestown. The company also carries ¾-inch #8 **bronze screws**.

Martin Marine Company, Route 236, Eliot, ME 03903. 207/439-1507. Here is the maker of the **Charles River Oarmaster,** the rowing unit used in the 18 ½-foot kayak shown and discussed in the text.

Durham Boat Company, RFD 2, Newmarket Road, Durham, NH 03824. 603/659-2548. This firm also makes **rowing units.**

Figure B-1. The 18 ½-footer with Charles River Oarmaster, offered by Martin Marine of Eliot, Maine. Since this picture was taken, the seat of the rowing machine was lowered two inches with very good results.

Index